# THE FUTURE OF EMPLOYMENT RELATIONS

P. B. Beaumont

SAGE Publications

London • Thousand Oaks • New Delhi

SAGE Publications Ltd
6 Bonhill Street
London EC2A 4PU

SAGE Publications Inc
2455 Teller Road
Thousand Oaks, California 91320

SAGE Publications India Pvt Ltd
32, M-Block Market
Greater Kailash - I
New Delhi 110 048

**British Library Cataloguing in Publication data**

A catalogue record for this book is
available from the British Library

ISBN 0 8039 7472 8
ISBN 0 8039 7473 6 (pbk)

**Library of Congress catalog card number 95-70198**

Typeset by Photoprint, Torquay, Devon
Printed in Great Britain at the University Press,
Cambridge

# THE FUTURE OF
# EMPLOYMENT RELATIONS

To Pat, Piers and Josceline

# CONTENTS

# ACKNOWLEDGEMENTS

Many academic and practitioner colleagues and friends have contributed over the years to the development of the material presented in this book. However, there are three individuals in particular who deserve a special mention and word of thanks for their contribution here. First, Tom Kochan (MIT) for his willing role in discussing so many of the themes and issues addressed in this work. Despite the best efforts of both Kathy and Pat to have us 'forget work', we have managed to talk through a great deal of this material over a considerable period of time. Indeed, many of the arguments here have strong parallels with Kochan's recent book (with Paul Osterman), *The Mutual Gains Enterprise* (Cambridge, Mass., Harvard Business School Press, 1994). Second, Richard Harris (University of Portsmouth), with whom I have collaborated on a number of research studies extending over more than ten years. This collaboration has been both enjoyable and informative, with much of our joint work underlying a good deal of the material presented here. And third, Peter Richards (Director of ACAS Wales), who has provided an 'important reality check' on my work through numerous discussions and his role in facilitating access to many other practitioners. Only Peter knows the full extent to which I am in his debt for some of the material presented here.

Finally, I am grateful to Mrs Eithne Johnstone, my long-suffering secretary, who has with typical good humour and efficiency produced a readable manuscript out of a jumble of drafts, revisions and notes which threatened to overwhelm us both at various stages in this particular endeavour.

The author and publishers wish to thank the following for permission to use copyright material:

Blackwell Publishers for Table 6.2 from D. Marsh, 'Public opinion, trade unions and Mrs Thatcher', *British Journal of Industrial Relations*, 28, 1 (1990), pp. 59–60;

BSA Publications Ltd and the authors for Table 6.1 from D. Marsden and M. Thompson, 'Flexibility agreements and their significance in the increase in productivity in British manufacturing since 1980', *Work, Employment and Society*, 4, 1 (1990), p. 90;

Cornell University Press for material for section 2 of Table 2.5 from L. Turner, *Democracy at Work* (1991), pp. 113–14;

André Deutsch Ltd for Table 1.4 from R. Taylor, *The Future of the Trade Unions* (1994), pp. 43–8;

The Economist Intelligence Unit for Table 7.3 from 'European labour costs hold steady', *Business Europe*, 19 September (1994), p. 2;

Financial Times for Table 8.1 from 'New competitiveness initiatives', *Financial Times*, 25 May (1994), p. 11;

Irish Congress of Trade Unions for Table 8.6 from *New Forms of Work Organisation: Options for Unions* (1990), p. 44;

MIT Press for Table 5.3 from C. Bean and J. Symons, 'Ten years of Mrs T', in *NBER Macroeconomics Annual* (1989). Copyright © 1989 National Bureau of Economic Research and Massachusetts Institute of Technology;

National Institute of Economic and Social Research for Table 5.1 from G.F. Ray, 'Labour costs in OECD countries, 1964–1975', *National Institute Economic Review*, 78 (1976), p. 58; and Table 5.2 from S.J. Prais, 'Economic performance and education: the nature of Britain's deficiencies', in National Institute of Economic and Social Research Discussion Paper 52 (1993), p. 9;

Organisation for Economic Co-operation and Development for Table 5.8 from *OECD Employment Outlook*, July (1993), p. 121. Copyright © 1993 OECD; and Introduction Table A from *OECD Employment Outlook*, July (1994), pp. 184–5. Copyright © 1994 OECD;

The Paper Federation of Great Britain for data included in Tables 6.6, 6.7, 6.8;

Joel Rogers for Table 2.4 from Richard B. Freeman and Joel Rogers, 'Who speaks for us? Employee representation in a nonunion labor market', in B.E. Kaufman and M.M. Kleiner (eds), *Employee Representation: Alternatives and Future Directions* (1993), Industrial Relations Research Association, p. 16;

Routledge for Table 2.6 from C. Brewster, 'European HRM: reflection of, or challenge to, the American concept', in P.S. Kirkbride (ed.), *Human Resource Management in Europe* (1994), pp.

65–6; Table 1.2 from R.J. Adams, 'Industrial relations under liberal democracy: North America in comparative perspective', in R. Bean, *Comparative Industrial Relations*, 2nd edn (1994), p. 78; Table 5.6 from C. Hendry, *Human Resource Strategies for International Growth* (1994), p. 145.

Every effort has been made to trace all the copyright holders but if any have been inadvertently overlooked the publishers will be pleased to make the necessary arrangement at the first opportunity.

# INTRODUCTION

The 1980s and the 1990s (at least to date) have been a 'tough' period of time for unions in many advanced industrialized economies. Sizeable falls in union membership have been recorded in a number of countries in response to a variety of influences, such as changes in the product market environment, changes in labour market conditions, the introduction of government legislation and changing employer attitudes and practices.

In some cases this union decline has been accompanied by a decline in the role and influence of collective bargaining. The position in these countries is very different from that in the 1970s, when an influential ILO study reported that:

> There can be little question about the broad acceptance which collective bargaining has gained in most industrialised countries. Speaking quite generally, one might say that collective bargaining has become so firmly established in the past three to four decades that it is sometimes regarded as synonymous with, or as constituting the essence of, the prevailing system of industrial relations. Nothing could be more revealing of the virtual identity between collective bargaining and the industrial relations system in certain countries than the comprehensive report of the Canadian Task Force on Labour Relations: the report is entitled *Canadian Industrial Relations*, but its contents are devoted almost entirely to collective bargaining and its key institutional components.[1]

Admittedly a declining role for collective bargaining is anything but a feature of all advanced industrialized economies at the present time. This fact is illustrated by the contents of Table A. In general the table suggests that the role of collective bargaining, at least at present, is most under threat in systems of industrial relations with the following features: (1) a strong, almost exclusive, union reliance on collective bargaining; (2) a traditionally adversarial collective bargaining process; (3) decentralized collective bargaining arrangements; and (4) the absence of mechanisms for extending the results and outcomes of collective bargaining. In this book the concentration is very much on a system of industrial relations (Britain) with these particular characteristics. That is, we are looking at a national system where collective bargaining is currently declining, and the concern or concentration is on the questions: what are the options for replacing collective bargaining, and how can this be achieved?

However, this examination of the British system is potentially instructive for a number of other systems. This is because, firstly, our analysis will pay a great deal of attention to the question of whether human resource management (HRM) has contributed to the decline of collective bargaining, and whether it has the potential to replace collective bargaining. This question is in no sense unique to Britain, as HRM practices are being introduced in many countries as part of a general employer desire for more

Table A  *Union density and collective bargaining coverage, selected OECD countries, 1980 and 1990 (per cent)*

| Country | 1980 | | 1990 | |
|---------|------------------|-----------------------------------|------------------|-----------------------------------|
|         | Union density | Collective bargaining coverage | Union density | Collective bargaining coverage |
| Australia | 48.0 | 88 | 40.4 | 80 |
| Canada | 36.1 | — (37 in 1985) | 35.8 | 38 |
| Finland | 69.8 | 95 | 72.0 | 95 |
| France | 17.5 | 85 | 9.8 | — (92 in 1985) |
| Germany | 35.6 | 91 | 32.9 | 90 |
| Great Britain | 50.4 | 70 | 39.1 | 47 |
| Japan | 31.1 | 28 | 25.4 | 23 |
| Netherlands | 35.3 | 76 | 25.5 | 71 |
| Portugal | 60.7 | 70 | 31.8 | 79 |
| Spain | 25.0 | — (67 in 1985) | 11.0 | 68 |
| USA | 22.3 | 26 | 15.6 | 18 |

*Source*: OECD *Employment Outlook*, July, 1994, pp. 184–5.

decentralized structures and more flexible working practices. As a consequence, unions in virtually all advanced industrialized economies are having to face the question of how to respond to such practices. Indeed the ILO World Labour Report for 1992 argued that the general union response to HRM has been inadequate to date, as a result of technical inadequacies and/or ideological reservations.[2]

The second point to make here is the possibility that a declining role for collective bargaining may increasingly characterize other national systems in the future. In relation to Table A the point was made that collective bargaining coverage has held up much better in relatively centralized systems of industrial relations. However, in a number of these countries, such as Finland, Germany and Sweden, there are increased employer demands for more decentralized bargaining arrangements. If these demands come to fruition then there is a very real possibility that the overall level of collective bargaining coverage will begin to decline. If this is the case then some of the issues which have been explored here in the British context may become of increasing relevance and importance to these other systems.

## THE BRITISH CASE

The traditional centrepiece of the British industrial relations system, in common with that of a number of other countries, has for long been a relatively adversarial, arm's-length collective bargaining relationship between unions and management. This relationship has essentially sought to determine and regulate the terms and conditions of employment, particularly those matters where some element of conflict is alleged to exist between employees (unions) and management.

However, collective bargaining has been anything but a constant over time. The 1960s and 1970s saw the outcomes of collective bargaining increasingly challenged by the introduction and operation of incomes policies, and the 1970s and 1980s witnessed the process of collective bargaining being increasingly subjected to legal regulation, while in the same years there was a strong trend towards the decentralization of collective bargaining at the individual company and plant levels. There have also been occasional reviews and proposed reforms of collective bargaining, most notably the well-known report of the Donovan Commission in 1968, which recommended more procedural regulation of collective bargaining at the plant and company level via an enhanced recognition and support of the roles of both shop stewards and the personnel management function. In addition, there have been periodic attempts made over time to supplement collective bargaining by the establishment of practices and arrangements designed to address issues in which employee (union) and management interests were perceived to be less ones of conflict and more ones of mutual interest. Initiatives along these lines have variously included profit-sharing schemes, joint consultative committees, joint health and safety committees, organization development and quality of work life initiatives, union directors on company boards, etc.

Before the 1980s and 1990s these changes, reviews and supplementary mechanisms never, however, sought to challenge one central belief of all the actors involved in the industrial relations system, namely, that collective bargaining was and should remain the centrepiece of the national industrial relations system. This is well evidenced by the fact that when the Advisory Conciliation and Arbitration Service (ACAS) was put on a statutory basis in 1976 it was charged with the task of improving industrial relations, with the major route to this improvement (at least to the early 1990s) being the extension and development of collective bargaining. By the beginning of the 1990s, however, the growth of the non-union employment sector had mounted a major challenge to the central role of collective bargaining. The results of the third National Workplace Industrial Relations Survey, for example, revealed that:

> Over the whole sample 54 per cent of employees were covered by collective bargaining in 1990. When grossed up to the population of employees covered by the sample this amounted to some 8.4 million out of a total of 15.3 million. As the 6.6 million employees excluded from our survey population – essentially those in small workplaces – are generally much less likely to be covered, *it is clear that collective bargaining directly affected only a minority of employees in Britain.*[3] [my emphasis]

Prior to this finding an earlier survey had reported that the scope or subject matter of collective bargaining had declined noticeably in the years 1980–4, although this process appeared to have been checked in the period 1984–90.[4] Nevertheless, one commentator has observed that 'it is now clear that in the course of the 1980s the coverage of collective bargaining has contracted substantially, that the scope of bargaining has narrowed, that the depth of union involvement has diminished, and that organizational security offered to unions by employers has deteriorated.'[5]

The decline in the coverage of collective bargaining, and the associated declines in union membership, density and recognition in the 1980s, and into the 1990s, has prompted a great deal of academic discussion and analysis of the reasons for, or causes of, this decline. Prominent in these discussions have been two questions concerning human resource management (HRM), namely (1) what (if any) role has HRM played in bringing about the decline of collective bargaining, and (2) can HRM replace collective bargaining as the centrepiece of the national industrial relations system?

There are few informed commentators who would, at least on the basis of the evidence to date, answer 'Yes' to the second question. Indeed the concern about the decline of collective bargaining is compounded by the observation that no clear-cut, coherent set of alternative arrangements (such as HRM) has, as yet, emerged in the non-union employment sector. Again to quote from the third National Workplace Industrial Relations Survey:

> Employee relations in non-union, industrial and commercial workplaces had relatively few formal mechanisms through which employees could contribute to the operation of their workplace in a broader context than that of their specific job. Nor were they as likely to have opportunities to air grievances or to resolve problems in ways that were systematic and designed to ensure fairness of treatment. Broadly speaking, no alternative models of employee representation – let alone a single alternative model – had emerged as a substitute for trade union representation.[6]

In short, there appears to be something of an institutional vacuum or gap in the growing, non-union employment sector in Britain at the present time. If one believes that any and all industrial relations systems should be based and evaluated on a concern for both efficiency and equity[7] then there would appear to be a strong *a priori* case for this institutional vacuum to be filled.

The questions then become how and with what should this gap be filled?

## THE QUESTION OF REPLACEMENT

In seeking to answer these questions one can identify at least three broad sets of issues that need to be addressed. The first is a debate about the desirability and feasibility of two broad, alternative models for the national industrial relations system: (1) a single centrepiece model, such as collective bargaining has traditionally provided in the past, or (2) a 'diversity' model, in which a variety of institutional arrangements co-exist, with no one set of arrangements dominating the system. At the present moment, collective bargaining remains important in the public sector, with more than three-quarters of the workforce there being covered by such arrangements. Collective bargaining also remains important in selected (predominantly older) industries, companies and plants in the private sector. But it is undoubtedly the private sector that is central to the debate about the desirability and feasibility of a diversity model of industrial relations.

The second set of questions and issues then becomes: what are the leading potential candidates for inclusion in a private sector diversity model? Broadly speaking, one can envisage the following contenders:

1   the human resource management approach, with its focus on consultation, involvement and information-sharing practices centred upon the individual employee or groups of employees;

2   collective bargaining either in its traditional form or with more of an emphasis on a joint problem-solving approach and orientation; and

3   the introduction of an alternative set of institutional arrangements, such as works councils.

The above are not necessarily mutually exclusive alternatives, in that one can envisage considerable potential overlap between them. For instance, one recent publication has argued that the individual employee orientation of HRM should not lead to a neglect of the collective aspects of employee relations;[8] they can and should be viewed as compatible and complementary in nature. Indeed, one of the issues explored in a later chapter is the extent to which HRM is being adopted in the union, as opposed to non-union, employment sector.

The third set of issues to be considered in any broad-ranging review of the British industrial relations system is the extent to which public policy should assist the take-up of one or more of the above candidates. That is, should one let the three potential candidates essentially 'fight it out' among themselves, with the most appealing and successful one being the one that will be increasingly adopted throughout the system on a voluntary basis? In other words, can and should one simply let competitive market forces naturally diffuse the individual set (or mix) of arrangements that best fit the particular needs of the parties in their individual circumstances? Alternatively, does public policy have a role to play?

This debate about the route to change needs to be seen in the light of two particular observations. The first is the view that Britain has essentially lacked a positive industrial relations policy in the last fifteen years or so. As Bill Daniel has noted:

> The chief criticism to be made of government industrial relations policy over the past decade is that there has been no policy in any positive sense of the term. Government action has not been inspired by any vision of what types of institutional arrangements are desirable for regulating the relationship between the employer and the employed. In short, it has been clear what the present government does not like but not at all clear what it would like to put in its place. It does not like trade unions. It does not like collective bargaining. ... Those articles of faith have equipped it well to lead a crusade against the status quo but not to introduce new arrangements more appropriate to the changing nature of industry and the workforce.[9]

The second observation is a recognition of the fact that the business community is generally opposed to the notion of more government regulation of the labour market, while at the same time other individuals have questioned the extent to which many existing regulations in the labour market have successfully achieved their objectives.

A rather different perspective needs to be inserted into this sort of debate, namely a fuller recognition of the fact that the notion of public policy is broader than that of regulation, with the latter's implied 'negative connotations' of legislation, bureaucracy, in-spectorates, adversarial court proceedings, etc. Indeed, at the present time there are some public policy measures and instru-ments of the type envisaged here actually in place in the industrial relations arena. For example, tax incentives have been provided to stimulate the adoption of employee share ownership schemes (one of the few 'positive' aspects of recent Government industrial relations policy), while ACAS has established joint working party arrangements to try to move highly adversarial union–manage-ment relationships in more of a joint problem-solving direction. Unfortunately, measures of this kind have not received the attention they deserve in debates about the role of public policy in the industrial relations sphere, which have been excessively dominated by the notions of legislation and enforcement. In short, the rather simple dichotomy 'legislation vs deregulation' needs to be recognized as a very limited debate, with much more attention being given to the question of the *nature*, as opposed to the extent, of public policy intervention in industrial relations. This is a theme that will be returned to at various points in the book.

This book is primarily concerned with discussing the declining role of collective bargaining as the traditional centrepiece of the British industrial relations system, and considering the various options for filling the resulting institutional gap or vacuum that has emerged. The motivation for writing the book was essentially twofold. First, and most obviously, is the belief that the above theme will (and should) increasingly occupy the agenda of industrial relations academics, practitioners and policy-makers throughout the 1990s. Secondly, in common with others,[10] I think it is desirable that at least some single, integrated teaching courses should exist on the employment or employee–management rela-tionship broadly defined. Such a course should cover both the union and the non-union sectors, and both industrial relations and HRM material. The need for such a course is particularly evidenced by the fact that the existing data do not support (see particularly Chapters 3 and 4) any simple teaching dichotomy along the lines of treating industrial relations as the study of collective bargaining in the union sector and HRM as the study of employee relations in the non-union sector. And hopefully the central theme addressed in this book can constitute a useful organizing device or framework (i.e. where are we coming from and going to?) that permits the presentation of a relatively broad set of material concerning the employment relationship within the confines of a single course.

## THE PLAN OF THE BOOK

Chapter 1 looks at collective bargaining as the traditional centre-piece of the British industrial relations system. It examines a variety of individual themes, such as the essential nature and strengths of collective bargaining, its various effects, some criticisms of its role and performance, and its changing nature over time. In Chapter 2 the subject of human resource management is introduced, with particular attention being given to its potential to both undermine and replace collective bargaining. The non-union employment sector is the subject of Chapter 3, where differing management attitudes towards union representation are examined, together with the implications of such attitudes for the adoption of HRM practices. In Chapter 4, attention is turned to the union sector of employment, where both union attitudes towards HRM practices and the organizational adoption of HRM practices are examined. Chapter 5 returns to the concern about an institutional vacuum emerging in the system. And here we examine some of the potential costs of this vacuum, and seek to generate some insights concerning how to fill this vacuum that are drawn from previous attempts to establish arrangements designed to complement collective bargaining. In Chapter 6 we return to the subject of collective bargaining and examine how it can potentially 'save itself' by becoming more of a joint problem-solving process. Chapter 7 poses the question of what can we learn from abroad by considering the potential for adopting some sort of works council model borrowed from Germany. Finally, in Chapter 8 we seek to draw together the major findings and lessons of the previous chapters and outline some of the changes that the various actors in the system will need to consider seriously if the existing institutional vacuum is to be closed.

## A PERSONAL STATEMENT

In any book concerning an important, but highly controversial, subject it is inevitable that a good deal of prescriptive material will be presented. As a consequence it seems only appropriate to indicate from the outset some of the leading normative assumptions, beliefs and propositions that underpin much of the material presented here. The major ones involved here may be listed as follows:

1  Any industrial relations system must be evaluated according to both efficiency and equity considerations.
2  Some degree of conflict is inevitable in the employment relationship.
3  HRM has rather more virtues than many academic commentators in Britain have conceded.
4  In practice it has been unfortunate, that industrial relations has come to be viewed as essentially the study of collective bargaining.
5  The longer-term viability of collective bargaining in Britain will require more of a joint problem-solving orientation.
6  The likelihood of a single, centrepiece model of industrial relations is extremely limited.
7  Competitive market forces are insufficient to close the institutional gap in the system.

Finally, it is important to emphasize that this book does not attempt to provide a detailed road map of the 'you must do this' sort for reforming the British industrial relations system. Rather the aim is to try to identify in a reasonably systematic fashion the key questions and issues to concentrate on, and the various possible options for answering these questions, with their differing strengths and weaknesses.

## REFERENCES

1  International Labour Office, *Collective Bargaining in Industrialised Market Economies*, Geneva, ILO, 1974, p. 12.
2  Cited in *European Industrial Relations Review*, 222, July, 1992, p. 31.
3  N. Millward, M. Stevens, D. Smart and W.R. Hawes, *Workplace Industrial Relations in Transition*, Aldershot, Dartmouth, 1992, p. 92.
4  Millward et al., *Workplace Industrial Relations*, pp. 249–55.
5  W. Brown, 'The contraction of collective bargaining in Britain', *British Journal of Industrial Relations*, 31 (2), 1993, p. 197.
6  Millward et al., *Workplace Industrial Relations*, p. 365.

7  J. Barbash, *The Elements of Industrial Relations*, Madison, University of Wisconsin Press, 1984.

8  J. Storey and K. Sisson, *Managing Human Resources and Industrial Relations*, Buckingham, Open University Press, 1993.

9  W.W. Daniel, 'Needed: a policy for industrial relations', *Policy Studies*, 11 (1), 1990, p. 25.

10  Storey and Sisson, *Managing Human Resources*.

# 1
# COLLECTIVE BARGAINING AND INDUSTRIAL RELATIONS

## INTRODUCTION

In the early 1950s Flanders observed that trade unions in Britain were mainly 'agencies for collective bargaining',[1] while in the early 1960s a Ministry of Labour publication saw collective bargaining as the 'normal means' of setting wages and working conditions.[2] These were by and large accurate statements at the time. In order to understand how such views and statements came about, this chapter examines the role of collective bargaining as the traditional centrepiece of the national system of industrial relations in Britain. The various individual topics covered in the chapter include the following: the origins and growth of collective bargaining, the essential nature of collective bargaining, some criticisms of its role, and its changing nature over time.

However, before turning to this material for the British system, we initially examine the issue of how industrial relations as a field of study became, at least in practice, overwhelmingly the study of collective bargaining.

## INDUSTRIAL RELATIONS AS THE STUDY OF COLLECTIVE BARGAINING

Most mainstream industrial relations researchers subscribe to one key normative premiss about their field or area of study, namely, that some degree of conflict is inherent in the nature of the employment relationship. There is, however, frequently some disagreement as to the sources of this conflict. To some this conflict arises from the fact of organizational hierarchy; others emphasize the differing objectives of employees and management; while yet others point to the role and influence of the broader structures of ownership and control in society at large. There is also some agreement on the central subject-matter of the area of the study, namely that the concentration is on institutional means for determining and regulating the terms and conditions of employment, or, in Dunlop's terms, the 'web of rules'.[3] However, Dunlop insisted that the 'web of rules' could be embodied in a variety of mechanisms, such as collective bargaining, arbitration awards, or statute law.

Admittededly, the nature of industrial relations research differs across national boundaries, with differences being apparent in what is studied and how it is studied. These differences frequently reflect (i) the differing importance of different mechanisms for determining and regulating the terms and conditions of employment in different systems, and (ii) the differing disciplinary backgrounds and training of leading researchers in different national systems. In many European countries, for instance, legal scholars have made much more of a contribution to industrial relations research than in the United States, because of the relatively important role of the State and statute law in Europe, which, in turn, has shaped the disciplinary training of the researchers. This being said, there is no question that collective bargaining has been the main preoccupation of industrial relations researchers in advanced industrialized economies, albeit the level at which collective bargaining was conducted and the extent to which it was legally regulated varied substantially across national boundaries. Admittedly, the particular aspects of the collective bargaining relationship that have been studied have shown some tendency to change over time. The contents of Table 1.1 indicate the changing research stream in Britain in the 1970s and 1980s – a changing emphasis that has been mirrored in a number of other national systems.

The contents of Table 1.1 notwithstanding, the reality is that over time industrial relations research in Britain, and indeed in other systems, has overwhelmingly concentrated on (1) the unionized sector of employment, (2) the collective bargaining relationship and (3) collectivities (i.e. the union and management representatives and specialists concerned with collective bargaining). As a consequence, the field of study has historically had little to say about

- non-union establishments;
- individual employees, in their employee, as opposed to union member, roles.

Moreover, the above approach in the unionized sector has made the all-powerful (albeit implicit) assumption that industrial relations changes resulted from industrial-relations-specific influences

Table 1.1    *Industrial relations research in Britain in the 1970s and 1980s*

---

*1970s research (union growth)*

- concentration on the union sector, collective bargaining relationship, the shop steward role, the individual plant level
- inductive case study approach widely used
- limited research from economists (except for the union-relative wage effect)
- little research on management role, except on the personnel function and degree of centralization/decentralization of industrial relations decision-making in multinational corporations
- EC membership and the 'social contract' stimulating an interest in 'industrial democracy' and 'corporatism' (comparative or cross-country research encouraged here)

*1980s research (union decline)*

- more research on management function (extending beyond the personnel function), and more attention to the corporate levels of decision-making
- more survey-based research from economists looking at union impacts beyond that of simply wages
- the beginnings of research on the non-union sector
- the introduction of new technology and flexible working arrangements increasingly popular topics
- research on reasons for union decline (largely by economists)
- the question of whether shop stewards had been 'incorporated' into the management way of doing things a subject of considerable debate
- more comparative research to assess degree of divergence/convergence between national systems

---

*Source*: P.B. Beaumont, 'Major research issues facing industrial relations in the 1990s: the British case', in Harry C. Katz (ed.), *The Future of Industrial Relations*, Cornell University: Institute of Collective Bargaining, New York State School of Industrial and Labor Relations, 1991, pp. 35–7.

that were very largely under the control of the specialist industrial relations representatives on the union and management sides.

There are two key questions to ask about the above set of statements. First, how did the above position come about? And secondly, why has it been increasingly viewed as a somewhat unsatisfactory state of affairs? The most obvious answer to the first question is simply the point stressed in the preface, namely that 'collective' bargaining was the traditional centrepiece of the national system of industrial relations in Britain, and indeed in many other countries. In other words, the research concentration very much mirrored organizational practice and reality. This can perhaps be illustrated by considering how industrial relations managers in Britain would have responded to the question 'How good are industrial relations in your organization?' Throughout the 1970s their answers to this question, if positive, were likely to have taken the following form:

1  Industrial relations are 'good' because I have a good collective bargaining relationship.
2  This good collective bargaining relationship is indicated by the relative absence of industrial action and by wage increases that are essentially in line with productivity increases and/or the organization's ability to pay.
3  This good collective bargaining relationship is due to the existence of comprehensive procedural agreements and a good personal rapport between myself and the shop stewards and union officials.

In short, the emphasis was on the goals of stability and predictability, with the route to these goals being essentially that of 'sharing power' with the unions.[4] By 'shadowing' this sort of practitioner perspective, industrial relations researchers traditionally provided a useful and sizeable perspective on the nature of the employment relationship, albeit with certain gaps and limitations in knowledge always present.

However, as fundamental changes in the product market and resulting changes in organizational practice increasingly undermined the above practitioners' view (that is, it became part of the story, but not anything like the full story), industrial relations as a field of study seemed to provide a much less sizeable and useful perspective on the employment relationship. The major challenges to both traditional industrial relations practice and research in the 1980s were as follows:[5]

1   the growth of the non-union employment sector, together with the emergent perception of certain leading non-union firms as the pace-setters (that is, potential role models) for innovative employee relations;

2   the increased realization that industrial relations changes were being driven by larger corporate level decisions (for example, competitive strategy, mergers, restructuring), whose processes took very limited account of industrial-relations-specific considerations; and

3   the emergence of new employment practices in which the individual employee, rather than the trade union, was the central focus of attention.

And these particular organizational-level changes seemed to be more quickly picked up and reflected in the HRM literature than in the industrial relations literature. It is the challenge that HRM presented to both the practice and the theory of industrial relations that will be explored in Chapter 2. However, in the remainder of this chapter we concentrate on the role of collective bargaining as the traditional centrepiece of the national system in Britain.

## THE ORIGINS AND GROWTH OF COLLECTIVE BARGAINING

In the late nineteenth century collective bargaining was disproportionately concentrated in two groups of industries.[6] Firstly, in the so-called skilled trades (for example engineering, shipbuilding, building, furniture-making and printing), where collective bargaining had largely grown out of the 'autonomous enforcement of trade union regulation', the latter being concerned with restricting entry to the skilled grades of labour and mutual insurance. And the second group of industries in which collective bargaining was centred was the piecework industries, such as coal-mining, iron and steel, cotton textiles, and boot and shoe manufacture. In these industries it was the interest of both employers and unions in trying to establish a floor to wage competition that gave rise to collective bargaining. It was very largely the employer interest in regulating wage competition in the piecework industries that provided the basis for Flanders' well-known and important contention that the Webbs had ignored any employer role in establishing collective bargaining arrangements.[7]

Collective bargaining in these two groups of industries initially took place on a district or local area basis. In 1910 some 1,696 trade or district agreements were estimated to directly cover some 2,400,000 employees,[8] a figure very similar to that for union membership in that year. However, with the movement towards national or industry-based bargaining arrangements in the early decades of the twentieth century, the extent of collective bargaining coverage began increasingly to outpace the level of union membership.[9]

It was very largely employers and the government that took the lead in the movement towards industry-level collective bargaining. The motivation of some (but certainly not all) employers in this regard was essentially threefold. Firstly, to minimize wage competition in the industry; secondly, to avoid individual employers being picked off and 'whip-sawed' via industrial action; and thirdly, to maintain the strength of managerial prerogative in the individual employment establishment. The latter involved the scope or subject-matter of joint negotiation being largely confined to wages–hours matters, the only matters that could realistically be settled by such relatively centralized arrangements. As to the government role, Flanders has commented that 'the Conciliation Act of 1896 can best be regarded as the turning point in the attitude of governments to collective bargaining, the first unambiguous sign of their approval'.[10] More important, however, was the pressure for union recognition and industry bargaining arrangements that the government brought to bear on employers' associations (in order to speed up wage-settlement decisions and avoid workforce disruption) during the two wartime periods. Bain's work, for instance, indicates that a disproportionate number of cases of white-collar recognition came about in the two wartime periods,[11] while histories of individual employers' associations document the exertion of government pressure to establish national bargaining arrangements in these periods of time.[12] By the end of the Second World War it has been estimated that some 15.5 million employees were covered by some form of national bargaining arrangements.[13]

In summary, the pattern of growth and development of collective bargaining in Britain in the period from 1910 through to the 1950s was characterized by the following key features:

1   There was a movement towards national or industry-based bargaining.
2   Collective bargaining coverage was considerably greater than that of union membership.
3   The scope of bargaining was relatively narrow, being confined largely to disputes procedures and wages–hours matters.
4   Influential employers' associations were subject to considerable government pressure to grant union recognition and establish national bargaining arrangements during the two wartime periods. As a result, the growth of union membership, recognition and collective bargaining coverage was disproportionately concentrated in these short, atypical periods of time.

Why the gap between collective bargaining coverage and union density? To answer this question one needs to distinguish between the *indirect* and *direct* coverage of collective bargaining. The former is essentially an inter-organizational phenomenon whereby non-union employers adopt wage-levels collectively bargained for in other firms. This may be done voluntarily, in order to try and minimize any employee interest in union representation, although in some periods of time in Britain industry-level collectively bargained wages have been extended by law and regulation to non-union establishments in the relevant industry.[14] When we concentrate only on the direct coverage notion the gap between collective bargaining coverage and union density is essentially an intra-organizational, phenomenon arising from the fact that, in the absence of closed shop arrangements, not all employees in a recognized bargaining unit will join a union.

It has been shown that total union membership, in Britain and elsewhere, has varied over time according to business cycle influences, such as changes in money wages, changes in prices, the level of and changes in unemployment, etc.[15] Has collective bargaining coverage exhibited a similar pattern of variation over time? The short answer is that we do not know, as the necessary data to investigate the question comprehensively are not available. Broadly speaking, however, one might reasonably expect an essentially similar pattern of change, although with one major qualification to be attached. That is, collective bargaining coverage (at least in the direct coverage sense) will arguably change rather less than union membership over time, as it is *jobs* (in the recognized bargaining unit) that are organized in the former case, and not *employees*, as in the latter case. In short, collective bargaining coverage is likely to be less cyclically sensitive than is the case with union membership.

How big is the gap between the two measures of union organization at any point in time? In the late 1960s one estimate put the difference at around 35 per cent,[16] and in the early 1970s it was reported to be some 23 per cent,[17] while figures in the 1984 and 1990 Workplace Industrial Relations Surveys[18] indicate a difference of 13 per cent and 6 per cent respectively. Although the difference appears to have narrowed over time, it is essential to recognize that the data sources underlying these figures are not always strictly comparable in nature; the coverage figures reported by Brown,[19] namely 65 per cent in 1968, 72 per cent in 1973, 64 per cent in 1984 and 47 per cent in 1990, certainly suffer from this particular problem. Finally, the contents of Table 1.2 indicate that a gap between collective bargaining coverage and union density is far from unique to Britain. In France, for instance, union density has fallen to around 10–12 per cent of the workforce, whereas the number of collective agreements at the sectoral and company level rose continuously in the period 1986–91;[20] legislation making negotiation compulsory on various subjects has been the key factor involved here.

## THE ESSENCE OF COLLECTIVE BARGAINING

One definition of collective bargaining is that it involves 'those arrangements under which wages and conditions of employment are settled by a bargain, in the form of an agreement made between employers or associations of employers and workers' organizations.'[21] To most mainstream industrial relations researchers this would be an unacceptably narrow view of the nature of collective bargaining. This is because it views collective bargaining as little more than the settling of substantive terms and conditions of employment at periodic points in time. Flanders, for example, has argued that collective bargaining is more than simply the collective equivalent and counterpart to individual wage bargaining, as it both *determines* and *regulates* the terms and conditions of employment.[22] The essence of Flanders' argument was strongly influenced by Chamberlain's view that collective bargaining involved:[23]

1  a marketing function which determined the basic substantive terms and conditions of employment at periodic points in time;

2  an industrial government function, whereby the procedural conditions under which employees work are determined and administered; and

3  a method of management, whereby the views of employees and trade unions constitute an input to decision-making processes whose outcomes will have implications for their particular interests and concerns.

These differing functions of collective bargaining have important implications for the on-going analysis and discussion in

Table 1.2    *Estimates of collective bargaining coverage and union density, early 1990s*

| Country | Collective bargaining coverage (%) | Union density (%) |
| --- | --- | --- |
| Australia | 85 | 35–40 |
| Denmark | 95 | 85–90 |
| Sweden | 90+ | 90+ |
| Germany | 90 | 35 |
| Netherlands | 80 | 25–30 |
| Italy | 80+ | 65 |
| United Kingdom | 55 | 40–45 |
| Switzerland | 65 | 30–40 |
| France | 70–80 | 10 |
| Canada | 40–45 | 35–40 |
| USA | 20+ | 13–18 |
| Japan | 20–25 | 20–25 |

*Source*: R.J. Adams, 'Industrial relations under liberal democracy: North America in comparative perspective', reported in R. Bean, *Comparative Industrial Relations*, 2nd edn, London, Routledge, 1994, p. 78.

Britain, and other countries, about the impact of unions (via collective bargaining) on the performance of individual organizations and the economy and society as a whole. Those academics who concentrate their analysis on function 1 above (traditionally economists) tend to be concerned with what has been labelled the 'monopoly' face of unions.[24] That is, they look at the role of unions in raising wages above competitive levels, lowering productivity through the imposition of restrictive practices, etc. In contrast, those who emphasize functions 2 and 3 (traditionally mainstream industrial relations researchers) are more likely to be interested in the 'collective voice/institutional response' face of unionism.[25] That is, they look at the role of unions in reducing arbitrary management actions in the workplace, increasing the degree of equality between employees, enhancing the efficient flow of information to management concerning workforce preferences, substituting grievances ('voice') for the necessity to quit, etc. Table 1.3 provides a summary statement of some recent union impact studies in Britain.

There are a number of other perspectives that have been taken on the nature of collective bargaining. Bargaining theorists, for

Table 1.3 *Research concerning union impact in Britain*

---

1 Unionized workplaces pay higher wages than comparable non-union ones. This differential is particularly high when a pre-entry closed shop exists, where multiple unions are bargaining separately, and where the product market is uncompetitive.
2 The size of the union/non-union pay differential has fallen in the 1980s.
3 Unions have reduced the extent of wage inequality, and as unions declined in the 1980s so the extent of pay inequality increased.
4 Over the 1980s, unionized establishments, companies and industries on average experienced more productivity growth than their non-union counterparts.
5 There is a strong negative relationship between unionization and financial performance or profitability at the workplace, firm and industry levels.
6 There is no clear-cut, conclusive evidence concerning the relationship between unions and investment.

---

*Source*: D. Metcalf, 'Transformation of British industrial relations? Institutions, conduct and outcomes 1980–1990', Centre for Economic Performance, LSE, Discussion Paper, 151, 1993.

example, have sought to distinguish collective bargaining from other sorts of bargaining relationships.[26] The major points typically made in this regard are that in collective bargaining

- the parties have to continue to interact over the course of time, and thus have a vested (mutual) interest in the survival of the relationship. As a result they are more likely to act as 'satisfiers' rather than 'maximizers' (as would be the case in a one-off bargain);
- the bargainers are acting as organizational representatives, rather than being engaged solely in an interpersonal bargain, and, as a result, there is the potential for intra-organizational conflict spilling over into inter-organizational conflict; and
- the bargain is a multiple-item one, which enhances the capacity for concessions and trade-offs by contrast with single-item bargaining.

This particular perspective has yielded some useful insights into the nature of bargaining power in the collective bargaining relationship.

A second perspective has sought to identify the virtues and strengths of collective bargaining compared with alternative mechanisms (for example legislation, unilateral management action, individual bargaining) for determining and regulating the terms and conditions of employment. The leading points typically made in favour of collective bargaining tend to emphasize certain gains to management, such as reduced transaction costs (in comparison with individual bargaining), increased information concerning the wishes of the average (as opposed to the marginal) employee, an important vehicle for 'selling change' to the workforce at large, and (particularly by contrast with legislation) a flexible and adaptable set of arrangements that can accommodate to the highly diverse needs and changing circumstances of individual workplaces.[27]

It has always been widely recognized that collective bargaining arrangements vary quite markedly between different national systems of industrial relations. For instance, a comparison of traditional collective bargaining arrangements in Britain and the USA would typically highlight the following sorts of differences:

- Historically multi-employer bargaining at the industry level has been more important in Britain.

- The scope or range of subjects covered by collective bargaining was less in Britain.

- Bargaining occurs on an annual basis in Britain, whereas agreements of 2–3 years' duration are more common in the USA.

- Collective agreements are not directly enforceable in law in Britain, so that the distinction between 'conflicts of rights' (that is, over the interpretation of the agreement during its life) and 'conflicts of interest' (that is, on the establishment of a new agreement) is much less important in Britain.

However, collective bargaining in Britain and the USA does have at least one thing in common, namely that the collective bargaining process in general has been viewed as a relatively adversarial, arm's-length one. In contrast, collective bargaining in many other countries (for example Japan) has been viewed as much more of a co-operative, joint problem-solving, mutual gains, etc., type of approach.

This sort of distinction should be seen in the light of the work of Walton and McKersie.[28] According to Walton and McKersie, all union–management relationships are essentially mixed-motive relationships, in which there is the potential for both conflict and co-operation. This results in an overall bargaining relationship that has two key sub-processes. First, distributive bargaining, which involves conflict, with one party seeking to achieve gains at the expense of the other (that is, it is a fixed-sum game). This particular sub-process will involve a good deal in the way of bluffing, threats and pressure tactics, with bargaining power being a strong determinant of the outcomes reached. The contrasting sub-process is integrative bargaining, which seeks to ensure mutual gains (that is, it is a varying-sum game) in areas where the parties have common interests. This particular joint problem-solving orientation will be influenced by factors such as the willingness of the parties to share information and the level of trust between them.

In Britain, and indeed some other countries (for example the USA and Canada), there is a general perception that (1) most union–management relationships have been dominated by the distributive, rather than the integrative, sub-process most of the time; and (2) the strength of the former has tended over time to reduce still further the extent and influence of the latter. The question of how one can seek to bring about a change in this regard is an important but complex one, which is discussed at various points in this book (see especially Chapter 6). For the present, however, it is useful to note two important insights for this change process, which are related to two other sub-processes of bargaining identified by Walton and McKersie.

1   Whether any bargaining relationship at any point in time is dominated by the integrative or the distributive sub-process is likely to be strongly influenced by the larger historical bargaining relationship. This is what Walton and McKersie call attitudinal structuring, which involves an attempt to establish and maintain a particular desired form of longer-term working relationship between unions and management (that is, one closer either to the distributive or to the integrative end of the spectrum).

2   Attempts to move to a more integrative bargaining relationship are likely to raise 'political' difficulties and issues within both unions and management. Thus this proposition involves what Walton and McKersie have termed intra-organizational bargaining, the process of reconciling and accommodating different interests *within* each of the parties involved in the bargaining relationship.

## THE CRITICS OF COLLECTIVE BARGAINING

As was noted earlier, the traditional supporters of collective bargaining have typically emphasized (1) the 'industrial jurisprudence' and 'method of management' functions of the process (that is, the 'voice'/institutional response face of unionism) and (2) the flexibility and adaptability of the process when compared with other methods of determining and regulating the terms and conditions of employment. At the same time we have already noted some criticisms of the process, namely, those coming from those who emphasize the marketing function of collective bargaining (that is, the monopoly face of unionism) and a more system-specific concern, namely that the process may be relatively adversarial in nature (that is, overmuch dominated by the distributive sub-process).

There are also three other lines of criticism of collective bargaining that have been pursued. The first is the contention that union representation and collective bargaining are both unnecessary and undesirable. This sort of criticism is underpinned by a view of an organization as essentially a co-operative venture, in which for effective performance the goals of employees and management must be essentially aligned through the establishment of a 'healthy psychological contract'.[29] According to this line of argument, union representation and collective bargaining only result from a 'management failure' to provide job satisfaction for its employees; hence limiting employee job dissatisfaction will limit the employee demand for union representation and collective bargaining. Moreover, once established, collective bargaining introduces a third (outside) party (the union) into the employment relationship, which will further hinder attempts to align the goals of employees and the organization, with resulting adverse implications for the level of organizational performance and effectiveness. As we shall see in the next chapter, many commentators see such views as being the essence of HRM, hence they argue that HRM has the potential to undermine the role of collective bargaining.

A second very different line of criticism has come from radical scholars, who have argued that collective bargaining arrangements have essentially reinforced the status quo by not challenging the larger structures and patterns of ownership and control in society at large.[30] In essence, the contention is that collective bargaining has not constituted a major challenge to the extent of management control, but rather has reinforced the status quo through: (1) producing only marginal improvements in the terms and conditions of employment; (2) lowering rank and file expectations with regard to what is realistically negotiable; (3) making industrial conflict more manageable through the processes of procedural regulation; and (4) limiting the development of a genuine trade union consciousness orientated towards larger political, social and economic change. Individuals who hold such views are likely to be particularly critical of attempts to move collective bargaining towards more of a joint problem-solving orientation. This is because such a change would be viewed as involving the 'co-option' of the union, thus reducing still further the role of the union in challenging the extent of management prerogative. Such concerns will be noted at various points in later chapters.

Earlier we noted some of the major points made in favour of the process of collective bargaining. These points have typically been made by individuals who take essentially a pluralist view of the nature of society at large and business organizations in particular. Such individuals have variously argued that (1) trade unionism and collective bargaining are essential to the maintenance of a larger democratic society; (2) some degree of conflict is inherent in the nature of the employment relationship, but that such conflict can be accommodated and resolved via collective bargaining; and (3) it is the procedural functions (voice, due process) of collective bargaining that are particularly important. Although always in favour of the principle of collective bargaining, such individuals have periodically criticized some aspects of its practice. One relatively long-standing concern has been that the outcomes of collective bargaining may take inadequate account of the notion of the public or social interest in industrial relations.[31] Such a perspective has frequently involved such individuals' advocating the introduction of some form of incomes policy to ensure that the outcomes of collective bargaining can be reconciled with the larger needs of macro-economic performance.

One of the major claims made by supporters of collective bargaining has always been, as was noted earlier, that it is a very flexible and adaptive set of institutional arrangements. This was alleged to be one of the great strengths of the traditional (pre-Donovan Commission) industrial relations system of Britain.[32] Moreover, as we shall see, collective bargaining has certainly had to try and adapt to a number of changes in the industrial relations system prior to the 1980s, and it is only more recently that this process of adaptation seems to have faltered.

## THE CHANGING INDUSTRIAL RELATIONS SYSTEM OF BRITAIN

When asked to describe the leading features of the British industrial relations system in the years prior to the Donovan Commission (1965–8), any student of the subject would have made at least the following points:

1   It is a system based very largely on collective bargaining.
2   This collective bargaining is conducted predominantly at the industry level.

3   This collective bargaining process is a voluntary (or free) one, characterized by the relative absence of legal regulation.

Throughout the 1970s and (particularly) the 1980s it became abundantly clear that features 2 and 3 had changed markedly, but it was only as one entered the 1990s that it also became apparent that feature 1 was being called into question for the first time.

Before the growth of the non-union employment sector in the 1980s, the primacy of collective bargaining in the system had never been seriously challenged. At most there had been periodic attempts to introduce complementary or supplementary practices and arrangements, designed very largely to enhance the integrative side of the union–management relationship. Examples along these lines included joint consultative committees and profit-sharing schemes. The 1970s also saw discussion of (and some limited experiments with) union directors on company boards as a means of reaching beyond collective bargaining to provide a union input into strategic decision-making processes. In Chapter 5 we will review the success of these initiatives, and identify some of the key lessons to have emerged from experience with them.

In the 1970s, and more especially in the 1980s, the traditional, multi-employer, industry-level collective bargaining arrangements increasingly gave way to more decentralized bargaining arrangements at the individual company and plant levels. This pattern of change was very much led by management and associated closely with the processes of corporate restructuring, and seemed to be driven by the belief that changes in production and working methods could be most efficiently and effectively brought about by decentralized arrangements.[33] Admittedly there were some exceptions to this general trend. Industry-level collective bargaining has remained relatively important in the public sector, although less so than in the past.[34] Furthermore, some parts of the private sector remained committed to the traditional bargaining arrangements, particularly in industries characterized by small firm size, highly competitive product markets, regional concentration, etc.[35]

However, the strength of the general trend towards decentralization was unmistakable. For instance, some key figures drawn from the third National Workplace Industrial Relations Survey (private sector only) were as follows:[36]

1   National bargaining covered 16.3 per cent of the manual workforce in 1990 (24.3 per cent in 1984) and 7.0 per cent of the non-manual workforce in 1990 (10.8 per cent in 1984).

2   Plant-level bargaining covered 20.4 per cent of the manual workforce in 1990 (25.8 per cent in 1984).

3   Company-level bargaining covered 29.4 per cent of the non-manual workforce in 1990 (16.4 per cent in 1984).

The much-reduced role of multi-employer, industry-level bargaining in Britain in the 1970s and 1980s was manifested in a number of ways. Initially in the 1970s it largely took the form of two-tier bargaining, with national agreements becoming very much minimum-rates agreements that were extensively supplemented by plant-level bargaining. In the paper and board industry, for example, some 72 per cent of the manual workforce covered by the national agreement were also covered by supplementary bargaining in 1978. However, over time more and more employers, particularly larger-sized ones, came out of employers' associations and established single-employer bargaining arrangements only. The membership of the Chemicals Industries Association, for example, has fallen from 341 in 1980 to 159 in 1991. As this process has gathered momentum the latest stage has been the actual abandonment of multi-employer industry bargaining. Brown and Walsh, for instance, report that at least sixteen major national bargaining groups, covering over a million employees, have been terminated since 1986.[37] These include those covering engineering, buses, banking, cotton textiles, independent television, food retailing, docks, cement and newspapers.

One major effect of the movement to decentralized bargaining arrangements has been the substantially reduced role and influence of employers' associations in the British industrial relations system; the total membership of all employers' associations included in the Annual Report of the Certification Officer in 1975 was 390,232, a figure down to 293,144 in 1991. This has been important for the unions, as they have lost 'their natural allies', who, as we saw earlier, were so important in facilitating the historical establishment of industry-level collective bargaining. As a consequence, the decision to recognize unions for collective bargaining purposes is now very much an individual employer decision relatively uninfluenced by peer-group pressure to follow industry traditions. The importance of this changed relationship is evidenced by the results of cross-country research which indicate that union membership levels in the 1980s held up much better in relatively centralized systems of industrial relations.[38]

The traditional system of industrial relations in Britain was invariably referred to as a voluntary system of collective bargaining. There were, as Flanders has demonstrated,[39] a number of myths associated with the term 'voluntarism': most notably the claim that employers and government played little role in establishing collective bargaining arrangements. This being said, there was no question that the traditional system was characterized by the relative absence of legal intervention. Admittedly the unions periodically sought the passage of legislation to offset (initially criminal and subsequently civil) liabilities imposed by judges in court decisions, but the unions always looked to this legislation as a source of immunities in law, rather than a set of positive legal rights; the high water mark of the union search for immunities was the passage of legislation in 1906.

The first major challenge to voluntary or free collective bargaining came in the 1960s with the introduction of various incomes policies designed to moderate the size of wage settlements in the interests of macro-economic stability.[40] However, during the 1970s (which also saw the operation of incomes policies) and 1980s (and into the 1990s) a more significant change to the system resulted from the passage of a substantial volume of employment legislation: some thirty pieces of employment legislation were passed in the decade of the seventies, compared to sixteen and five in the 1960s and 1950s respectively.[41] The first major piece of legislation introduced was the Industrial Relations Act 1971, which was modelled to a considerable extent on US legislation. This Act reflected the Government's belief that the unions had too much power, and that the balance of bargaining power needed to be pushed more in favour of employers; in this sense it sought to reform, rather than replace, collective bargaining. However, the unions effectively boycotted the legislation, and its resulting impact on the system was deemed to be relatively limited.[42] The major lessons of this experience, at least for a subsequent Conservative Government, were deemed to be the difficulty of curbing union power when unions are growing; the need to ensure that employers utilize the provisions of the legislation; and that a single piece of legislation risks acting as a rallying-point for union opposition.

This Act was repealed in 1974, with only the unfair dismissal provisions being retained. However, following entry into the EC, the Wilson–Callaghan Labour Governments passed a substantial body of employment legislation in the years 1974–9.[43] This legislation, which was considerably influenced by French and German practice, basically had two broad aims: (1) to provide a minimum set of rights for individual employees both during and at the end of the contract of employment; and (2) to reduce the extent of management prerogative and unilateral decision-making by requiring more joint consultation, discussion and negotiation about a broader range of subjects.

The third wave of legislation has been passed by the Conservative Government(s) in the years since 1979.[44] This period of time has seen a number of major pieces of employment legislation passed, which have had a variety of aims, most notably the removal of closed shop arrangements; a substantial reduction in the scope of union immunities in law; and an increased input from rank and file members into union decision-making processes. Table 1.4 lists some of the leading provisions in these various pieces of legislation.

The legislation since 1979, in contrast to the 1971 Act (with its essentially reformist approach), has been much more anti-union and anti-collective bargaining, in that it has sought to reduce the appeal to employees of such institutions, and increase the extent of management opposition to them, by constraining their range of permissible activities and hence their potential effectiveness. There is, however, considerable debate and disagreement among researchers as to whether the legislation has achieved its aims in this regard.[45] What is not in dispute, however, is the sort of change that has occurred in the system over time which is illustrated by the following quotations:

1  'Properly conducted, collective bargaining is the most effective means of giving workers the right to representation in decisions affecting their working lives.' (Donovan 1968, para. 212)

2  'Traditional patterns of industrial relations, based on collective bargaining and collective agreements, seem increasingly inappropriate and are in decline.' (Cm 1810, 1992, para. 1.15)[46]

In summary, it is clear that the multi-employer and voluntary basis of the traditional industrial relations system of Britain had

Table 1.4   *Some major pieces of employment legislation since 1979*

---

*1980 Employment Act*

- Picketing was to be limited to strikers in lawful strikes at their own place of work.
- Secondary action by strikes was made lawful only if it was concerned with contracts of employment, and was limited to the first supplier or customer of the goods and services of the employer in dispute in cases where the principal reason for the action was to prevent the supply of goods and services during the period of the dispute.
- Legal remedies were provided for workers to use against their trade unions if they were 'unreasonably excluded or expelled' from the union on the grounds of refusing to join a closed shop. This right was extended to cover not just employees with genuine religious convictions against closed shops but also to those who object 'on grounds of conscience or other deeply held personal conviction'.
- New closed shops were to be deemed lawful only where there was a majority support from employees for them in legally mandatory secret ballots where 80 per cent of those entitled to vote did so.
- The burden of proof was lifted from an employer that he had acted reasonably in dismissing an employee in a case of unfair dismissal. A worker had to be employed for two years to be able to bring an unfair dismissal case before an industrial tribunal, and not six months as had been the case under the 1975 Employment Protection Act.
- The trade union recognition provisions of the 1975 Employment Protection Act were repealed.
- Schedule 11 of the 1975 Act was repealed: this had enabled unilateral action by employees to secure pay rises from their employers to bring them up to the general level of recognized terms and conditions of other employees in the area.
- Financial aid was to be provided for trade unions that wanted money to assist in the holding of strike ballots and elections of union officials as well as ballots on union rule changes.

*1982 Employment Act*

- Section 14 of the 1974 Trade Union and Labour Relations Act was repealed, removing the legal immunity from trade unions for action in tort. This enabled, for the first time since 1906, the suing of a trade union in a court for punitive damages in an unlawful dispute. The trade union was made liable for any unlawful actions that had been authorized or endorsed by its specific trade union officials.

Table 1.4    *continued*

---

- Legal immunities were removed from trade unions where actions were taken that were not 'in contemplation or furtherance of a trade dispute'. A new and much narrower definition of a trade union dispute was introduced, to outlaw solidarity action by workers at home or abroad, as well as sympathy strikes or inter-union disputes.
- Further moves were made to limit the closed shop. All closed shops had to be balloted if they had not been in existence for five years, and an 85 per cent majority of those voting was needed to confirm their lawful existence. An employee could bring a joint claim against both the employer and the trade union for unfair dismissal in a closed shop where the legal requirements had not been met.
- 'Trade union only' commercial contracts were declared illegal.
- Trade unions and others organizing industrial action lost their legal immunities where they tried to force an employer to sign 'union labour only' contracts.

*1984 Trade Union Act*

- Provided for the holding of secret ballots for the direct election of trade union executives at least once every five years, where practicable by post but otherwise among their members in the workplace.
- A secret ballot had to be held before a trade union could call its members out on strike. If this was not done the union lost its immunity from civil action in the courts. A majority had to agree to the proposed strike, and the ballot had to be held no more than four weeks before the stoppage began.
- A secret ballot had to be held by the trade unions on holding political funds, to ensure members approved of the use of trade union finances for political purposes.

*1986 Wages Act*

- Abolished the Truck Acts, so that all manual workers had in future to be paid entirely in cash.
- Removed young workers under the age of twenty-one from the provisions of the Wages Councils designed to protect low-paid employees.

*1988 Employment Act*

- Abolition of all remaining legal protections for the post-entry closed shop. No strike was to be lawful that tried to enforce a closed shop.

Table 1.4  *continued*

---

- Trade unionists in a lawful strike who crossed picket lines to work could not be disciplined by their own trade union even if the majority of the employees concerned supported the strike.
- No trade unionist could be called out on strike without the holding of a secret ballot.
- All trade unionists had the right to a postal ballot in all union elections and pre-strike ballots.
- The Commission for the Rights of Trade Union Members was created, with the stated purpose of helping trade union members with legal advice and financial support.

*1989 Employment Act*

- Most laws discriminating between men and women in employment were repealed.
- The Training Commission was abolished, and its functions returned to the Department of Employment.

*1990 Employment Act*

- The abolition of the pre-entry closed shop was carried through by making it unlawful for an employer to refuse employment to a worker over the question of trade union membership.
- Trade union officials were required to repudiate or take responsibility for unofficial strikes.
- Legal immunities were removed from trade unions in any industrial action taken to support people dismissed selectively for taking part in an unofficial strike.
- All remaining forms of secondary action in disputes were made unlawful.

*1993 Trade Union Reform and Employment Rights Act*

- The check-off system (the automatic deduction of trade union membership dues by an employer from employees) was made unlawful unless each trade union member gave his or her written authorization every three years.
- Workers were given the right to join the trade union of their choice, which undermined the TUC's 1939 Bridlington Agreement that regulated which trade unions workers could join.
- All trade union pre-strike ballots were made postal, subject to independent scrutiny, with at least seven days' notice of action to be given by the trade union after the ballot result to enable the employer to prepare for it.

Table 1.4    *continued*

---

- Everybody who used public services was given the right to seek an injunction against a trade union to prevent the disruption of those services by unlawful industrial action.

- Everybody who worked more than eight hours a day for an employer became entitled to receive a clear written statement of terms and conditions of employment.

- The terms of reference of ACAS were changed so that it no longer had to promote and encourage collective bargaining.

- All Wages Councils were abolished and all minimum wage fixing for workers was ended.

- Industrial tribunals had their jurisdiction extended to cover breaches of employment contracts.

- All women were to enjoy a fourteen-week continuous maternity leave, with protection for pregnant women from unfair dismissal.

- Employers were allowed to offer trade unionists financial inducements to leave their unions.

- Protection was given under the law for workers who faced victimization and dismissal in health and safety cases where they sought to protect themselves and other workers from imminent danger.

---

*Source*: R. Taylor, *The Future of the Trade Unions*, London, Deutsch, 1994, pp. 43–8.

essentially gone by the end of the 1980s. But as one entered the 1990s it was also apparent that the real bedrock of the system, namely collective bargaining, was also being seriously called into question for the first time.

## SUMMARY

In this chapter we have looked in turn at the historical development of collective bargaining, its essential nature, and its alleged strengths and weaknesses, and have sought to locate it in the context of the changing system of industrial relations as a whole. However, in the course of the chapter we have identified certain individual themes that will be covered in more detail in subsequent chapters. Some of these leading themes are as follows:

- Employers' associations were prominent in helping to establish national-level collective bargaining in Britain. Does the decentralization of the system, and the resulting loss of authority and influence of employers' associations, mean that the unions have lost an important ally in the task of maintaining collective bargaining?

- If HRM is a route to enhanced employee job satisfaction, will this limit the future demand for union representation and collective bargaining?

- If traditional collective bargaining has been relatively adversarial in nature, has this enhanced management opposition to collective bargaining? Can this management opposition be reduced by making the process less adversarial in nature, without at the same time risking the co-option of unions?

These will be among some of the leading issues examined throughout this book.

## REFERENCES

1   A. Flanders, *Trade Unions*, London, Hutchinson, 1952, p. 76.
2   Ministry of Labour *Industrial Relations*, 3rd edn, London, HMSO, 1961, p. 3.
3   J.T. Dunlop, *Industrial Relations Systems*, New York, Holt, Rinehart and Winston, 1958.
4   J. Purcell, 'A strategy for management control in industrial relations', in J. Purcell and R. Smith (eds), *The Control of Work*, London, Macmillan, 1979, pp. 27–57.
5   T.A. Kochan, H.C. Katz and R.B. McKersie, *The Transformation of American Industrial Relations*, New York, Basic Books, 1986.
6   A. Flanders, 'Collective bargaining', in A. Flanders and H.A. Clegg (eds), *The System of Industrial Relations in Great Britain*, Oxford, Blackwell, 1954, pp. 260–72.
7   A. Flanders, 'The nature of collective bargaining', in A. Flanders (ed.), *Collective Bargaining*, Harmondsworth, Penguin, 1969, pp. 11–41.
8   Flanders, 'Collective bargaining', p. 275.
9   H.A. Clegg, *A History of British Trade Unions since 1889*, Vol. II: 1911–1933, Oxford, Clarendon Press, 1985, p. 571.
10   Flanders, 'Collective bargaining', p. 273.

11    G.S. Bain, *The Growth of White Collar Unionism*, Oxford, Clarendon Press, 1970.

12    E. Wigham, *The Power to Manage*, London, Macmillan, 1973.

13    P. Blyton and P. Turnbull, *The Dynamics of Employee Relations*, London, Macmillan, 1994, p. 182.

14    K.W. Wedderburn, *The Worker and the Law*, 2nd edn, Harmondsworth, Penguin, 1971, pp. 200–4.

15    G.S. Bain and F. Elsheikh, *Union Growth and the Business Cycle*, Oxford, Blackwell, 1976.

16    A. Flanders, *Collective Bargaining: Prescription for Change*, London, Faber, 1967, p. 13.

17    P.B. Beaumont and M.B. Gregory, 'The role of employers in collective bargaining in Britain', *Industrial Relations Journal*, 11 (5), 1980, p. 47.

18    N. Millward, M. Stevens, D. Smart and W.R. Hawes, *Workplace Industrial Relations in Transition*, Aldershot, Dartmouth, 1992, pp. 60, 93.

19    W. Brown, 'The contraction of collective bargaining in Britain', *British Journal of Industrial Relations*, 31 (2), 1993, p. 191.

20    *European Industrial Relations Review*, 225, 1992, pp. 27–9.

21    Ministry of Labour, *Industrial Relations*, p. 18.

22    Flanders, 'The nature of collective bargaining'.

23    N.W. Chamberlain, *Collective Bargaining*, New York, McGraw-Hill, 1951, p. 121.

24    R.B. Freeman and J.L. Medoff, *What Do Unions Do?* New York, Basic Books, 1984, p. 13.

25    Ibid., p. 13.

26    P.B. Beaumont, *Change in Industrial Relations*, London, Routledge, 1990, pp. 127–30.

27    International Labour Office, *Collective Bargaining in Industrialized Market Economies*, Geneva, ILO, 1974, pp. 12–13.

28    R.E. Walton and R.B. McKersie, *A Behavioral Theory of Labor Negotiations*, New York, McGraw-Hill, 1965.

29    E. Schein, *Organizational Psychology*, Englewood Cliffs, Prentice-Hall, 1965.

30    R. Hyman, *Industrial Relations: A Marxist Introduction*, London, Macmillan, 1974.

31    Flanders, *Collective Bargaining: Prescription for change*, pp. 19–27.

32    O. Kahn-Freund, 'Intergroup conflicts and their settlement', in Flanders (ed.), *Collective Bargaining*, 1967, pp. 59–85.

33    B. Towers, 'Collective bargaining levels', in B. Towers (ed.), *A*

*Handbook of Industrial Relations Practice*, 3rd edn, London, Kogan Page, 1992, pp. 167–84.

34   P.B. Beaumont, *Public Sector Industrial Relations*, London, Routledge, 1992.

35   P.B. Beaumont and A.W.J. Thomson, 'The structure of collective bargaining in Britain', in A. Bowey (ed.), *Managing Salary and Wage Systems*, 3rd edn, Aldershot, Gower, 1989, pp. 9–29.

36   *Industrial Relations Review and Report*, 548, November 1993.

37   W. Brown and J. Walsh, 'Pay determination in Britain in the 1980s: the anatomy of decentralization', *Oxford Review of Economic Policy*, 7 (1), 1991, p. 49.

38   R.B. Freeman, 'The changing status of unionism around the world', in W.-C. Huang (ed.), *Organized Labor at the Crossroads*, Kalamazoo, Michigan, Upjohn Institute for Employment Research, 1989, pp. 111–38.

39   A. Flanders, 'The tradition of voluntarism', *British Journal of Industrial Relations*, 12 (3), 1974. pp. 352–70.

40   Beaumont, *Change in Industrial Relations*, pp. 206–12.

41   B. Hepple, 'Individual labour law', in G.S. Bain (ed.), *Industrial Relations in Britain*, Oxford, Blackwell, 1983, p. 393.

42   A.W.J. Thomson and S.R. Engleman, *The Industrial Relations Act*, London, Martin Robertson, 1975.

43   See Hepple, 'Individual labour law'. Also R. Lewis, 'Collective labour law'.

44   K.J. Mackie, 'The legal background: an overview', in Towers (ed.), *A Handbook*, 3rd edn, 1992, pp. 295–321.

45   See, for example, R. Freeman and J. Pelletier, 'The impact of industrial relations legislation on British union density', *British Journal of Industrial Relations*, 28 (2), 1990.

46   Both cited in Brown, 'Contraction of collective bargaining', pp. 189, 190.

# 2
# COLLECTIVE BARGAINING AND HUMAN RESOURCE MANAGEMENT

## INTRODUCTION

The 1980s saw two important developments in many advanced industrialized economies. First, the levels of union density, recognition and collective bargaining coverage declined in a number of systems (see Introduction, Table A). Secondly, the concept of human resource management arrived from the United States and became a notable component of the language of many management practitioners. Are these two developments linked in the sense of the latter having contributed, at least in part, to the former? The debate surrounding this question is the central subject-matter of this chapter. However, here we largely confine ourselves to the leading *a priori* arguments and contentions that have been put forward. The presentation of some relevant empirical material is deferred until Chapters 3 and 4, when we examine the non-union and union sectors in turn. But before outlining the nature of the debate concerning this question, it is necessary to say a little more about the basic nature of HRM.

## WHAT IS HRM?

This deceptively easy question is in fact a difficult one to answer. You can probably get as many different answers as there are researchers in the subject area. To some it is simply a useful generic term for discussing a broad range of employee relations matters, including, but extending beyond, collective bargaining. For others the central message of the notion (and hence the leading test for its existence) is the need to develop a close, two-way relationship between an individual organization's competitive strategy and its internal industrial relations or employee relations policies and practices. However, to many industrial relations researchers, with their strong institutionalist tradition, it means the 'individualizing of industrial relations', with management focusing much more attention on the individual employee. For example, one recent publication took the following position:[1]

> HRM is taken as referring to the general package of measures designed to deliver workplace flexibility; employee involvement, commitment and identification with organizational objectives like total quality which are to be realized through team working; the individualization of pay through, for example, knowledge or skills-based remuneration; and new forms of direct communication like team briefings and quality circles.

One way into the subject area is to ask the question: what would an organization with a relatively well-developed set of HRM practices look like? Again, answers will vary somewhat, but many commentators are likely to subscribe, at least to a considerable extent, to the features set out in Table 2.1. This generic framework is obviously a highly idealized system, in the sense that one is unlikely to find many organizations with all these features in place at any one time. The questions then become which of these features are the priority ones and how many of them must be in place before one can say that a particular organization is pursuing an HRM approach? To date, a good deal of researcher attention has been given to feature (2), with the overwhelming judgement being that relatively few organizations have adopted a relatively strategic approach towards HRM.[2] In other words, there is relatively little evidence to indicate that many organizations have systematically incorporated HRM considerations into their strategic decision-making processes.

However, the specific question of whether HRM has contributed to the decline in collective bargaining tends to focus on a different feature of Table 2.1, namely feature (7). That is, the concern is whether an organization that emphasizes flexible work operations and concentrates its communications and participation initiatives on the individual employee will have adverse implications for the role of collective bargaining. This particular theme has been the subject of considerable debate and disagreement, the essence of which we turn now to consider.

Table 2.1   *An organization with a strong commitment to HRM*

1   The firm competes on the basis of product quality and differentiation as well as price.

2   Human resource considerations weigh heavily in corporate strategic decision-making and governance processes. Employee interests are represented through the voice of the human resource staff professionals and/or employee representatives consult and participate with senior executives in decisions that affect human resource policies and employee interests. In either case, employees are treated as legitimate stakeholders in the corporation.

3   Investments in new hardware or physical technology are combined with the investments in human resources and changes in organizational practices required to realize the full potential benefits of these investments.

4   The firm sustains a high level of investment in training, skill development, and education, and personnel practices are designed to capture and utilize these skills fully.

5   Compensation and reward systems are internally equitable, competitive and linked to the long-term performance of the firm.

6   Employment continuity and security is an important priority and value to be considered in all corporate decisions and policies.

7   Workplace relations encourage flexibility in the organization of work, empowerment of employees to solve problems, and high levels of trust among workers, supervisors and managers.

8   Worker rights to representation are acknowledged and respected. Union or other employee representatives are treated as joint partners in designing and overseeing innovations in labour and human resource practices.

*Source*: T.A. Kochan, 'Principles for a post-New Deal employment policy', Sloan School of Management, MIT, Working Paper, 5, 1992.

## THE DEBATE ABOUT HRM AND COLLECTIVE BARGAINING

Those commentators who argue that HRM can undermine and has undermined collective bargaining are likely to make the following sorts of points. Firstly, that HRM is very much led by line management, a fact which has adverse implications for the organizational status, influence and power of the personnel management function. The most extreme version of this view is that a division of labour is evolving within the management of organizations, whereby line management concentrate on individual employee relations, and the personnel function concentrates on collective (union-based) relations. But as the latter are of declining importance within organizations this means that the part of management that is most knowledgeable about, and well disposed towards, unions and collective bargaining is becoming less influential in management decision-making circles.

A second argument views the basic aim of HRM as being to produce a relatively close alignment between the aims of individual employees and those of the organization. More specifically it has been alleged that the communication and participation initiatives centred on individual employees will have the effect of increasing the extent of employee job satisfaction. And if this occurs it will limit the employee demand for union representation and collective bargaining, given the research that indicates that the demand for such representation arrangements tends to be triggered by the fact of job dissatisfaction.[3] In other words, this contention views HRM practices as being potentially important for firms seeking to maintain their non-union status over the course of time.

A third contention is more concerned with the adverse implications of HRM practices for unions and collective bargaining arrangements in the unionized sector of employment. The argument is again that HRM practices increase the level of employee job satisfaction, with the result that individual employees increasingly identify with the company and correspondingly identify less with the union. One of the major alleged effects of such a change is that the traditional role of the unions in raising and settling employee grievances with management would be substantially eroded. Underlying this basic line of argument is the so-called 'dual loyalty' hypothesis, which contends that there is essentially a trade-off between being a 'good' employee and being a 'good' union member, a relationship which has received only limited empirical support.[4] This particular line of argument also seems frequently to assume that more communication with individual employees must necessarily mean less communication with the unions.

A fourth, related, contention is that the movement towards flexible working practices, such as team work arrangements, will weaken the traditional importance of seniority in work allocation decisions and pit individual workers against each other (via the influence of peer pressure in teams).[5] As a result it has been alleged that the extent of managerial discretion will increase and that the ability of unions to challenge this increased management control effectively will be less, because the union has a membership that is increasingly divided.

These particular arguments and contentions have certainly not gone unchallenged. To many commentators HRM is unlikely to have played a major role in undermining collective bargaining in Britain in the 1980s for a number of reasons. The first argument that is likely to be put forward in this regard concerns the limited practice and application of HRM. In this particular case what is being contended is that the rhetoric about HRM is running well ahead of organizational practice and reality. In other words, it is conceded that collective bargaining has declined, but it is argued that this occurrence in Britain in the 1980s cannot have been due in large measure to HRM, because HRM practices are very thinly

Table 2.2   *Rhetoric vs reality: an illustration*

---

- There has been considerable concern about workplace health and safety in Britain in the 1980s. For instance, the level of major accidents rose sharply in the years 1981–5, while a recent report from the Health and Safety Executive (*Financial Times*, 9 February 1994) suggested that the costs of accidents and illness at work were equivalent to 2–3 per cent of GDP.

- In the same years there was a great deal of management rhetoric about the desirability of employee 'empowerment', and numerous best-practice management health and safety guides stressed the importance of spreading the sense of ownership of health and safety through training, communications and employee involvement initiatives.

- However, an examination of the panel data set of the third National Workplace Industrial Relations Survey revealed that
  (1) the proportion of establishments where management did not consult with the workforce about health and safety matters increased from 26.5 per cent in 1984 to 36.1 per cent in 1990; and
  (2) the establishments that had moved away from consultation in the years 1984–90 had the highest injury rates.

---

*Source*: P.B. Beaumont and R.I.D. Harris, 'Consultative document', *Occupational Safety and Health*, 23 (7), 1993, p. 51.

spread in both the union and non-union sectors of employment. The contents of Table 2.2 provide an illustrative example of the divergence between the rhetoric and the reality of HRM.

A second relevant line of argument involves the contention that HRM practices embody certain internal contradictions and tensions.[6] In other words, HRM does not involve a consistent and coherent set of employee relations practices. Although it is not always clear whether these internal inconsistencies are seen as inherent in HRM, as opposed to resulting from poor implementation practices, this line of argument would seem to suggest the possibility of finite limits to the extent to which HRM can undermine collective bargaining. These limits can potentially arise from two major sources. First, if management increasingly recognizes, through unfavourable experience, these internal weaknesses, limitations and inconsistencies, then there may well be a backlash against the approach. In other words, the already limited application of HRM practices will not go much further, as management will abandon the approach owing to the limited pay-off to be gained from the practices as a result of their internal contradictions. A second source of possible limits to the role of HRM in undermining collective bargaining may come from individual employees and union members. That is, the introduction of HRM practices may raise their expectations concerning job satisfaction, involvement, empowerment, etc.; but if these expectations are not fulfilled, this may result in an enhanced demand for, or commitment to, union membership and collective bargaining arrangements. In short, HRM practices that fail to deliver may prove to be counter-productive from the employer point of view and, as such, constitute a 'blessing in disguise' for the unions. A recent survey of union activity in Britain certainly revealed that the introduction of HRM practices in organizations had not resulted in a marked reduction in employee grievances.[7]

A third relevant argument is that, at least in principle, there is no necessary contradiction between HRM and collective bargaining. That is, HRM will not necessarily result in a declining role for collective bargaining, at least if the collective bargaining relationship is a relatively co-operative one. Indeed to some US commentators a joint problem-solving union–management relationship is an integral part of the larger human resource management set-up in a unionized organization.[8] This particular theme is pursued further in the next section.

## A CONTINGENCY-BASED RELATIONSHIP?

To some commentators the previous section's discussion is essentially a misplaced exercise, in the sense that it talks about the relationship between HRM and collective bargaining in very general terms. Instead, they would favour very much a contingency approach that would hold that whether HRM has a complementary (or negative) relationship with collective bargaining will critically depend on the particular circumstances of individual union–management relationships. The strength and value of this line of argument would seem to be indicated by the fact that empirical research has documented a list of both benefits and costs for unions in union–management co-operative initiatives. A listing of such benefits and costs is set out in Table 2.3.

The general thrust of the US literature seems to be that HRM will have a complementary relationship with collective bargaining, and hence the benefits to unions will outweigh the costs to

Table 2.3   *The potential benefits and costs to unions of union–management co-operation*

---

*The potential benefits*
- recognition from members for improvement
- greater participation and input in management decisions
- improved communications between union leaders and managers
- reduced day-to-day contract administration problems
- greater membership input into regular union activities and policies

*The potential costs*
- perceived co-optation by management
- undermining traditional roles of unions and collective bargaining
- heightened political conflict over leadership role
- increased uncertainty of re-election
- loss of member commitment and union influence

---

*Source*: W.N. Cooke, *Labor–Management Co-operation*. Kalamazoo, Michigan, Upjohn Institute for Employment Research, 1990, pp. 12–14.

them in those situations characterized by a relatively co-operative or joint problem-solving union–management relationship. This perspective raises the questions: what is the essence of a joint problem-solving union–management relationship, and what circumstances and factors can help bring it about? This is a matter we have already touched on in Chapter 1, and will certainly return to in more detail in later chapters (see Chapter 6 in particular). However, a few preliminary observations can usefully be put forward at this stage. The first point is to sweep away two very superficial views of the essence of joint problem-solving. In other words, we need to recognize what a joint problem-solving collective bargaining relationship does *not* involve. The two points to be noted here are as follows:

1   Joint problem-solving does not, and indeed should not, mean that all sources of conflict between unions and management are eliminated. Rather the essence of it is to ensure that any conflict in a particular area or aspect of the employment relationship does not drive out the potential for co-operation in other areas of the relationship.

2   Joint problem-solving does not mean the absence of an independent union agenda. In other words, it does not mean that the union agenda is simply the management agenda.

This second point can be pursued a stage further. There is often a perception that a management-led, comprehensive HRM approach in an individual organization leaves relatively little scope for an independent union agenda, particularly where the majority of individual employees have responded relatively positively to the approach. However, Adler's recent examination of the well-known New United Motors Manufacturing Inc. (NUMMI) in the US argues that, despite its comprehensive HRM approach, there was still considerable scope for the development of a more independent and powerful union agenda centring around (i) the ergonomic qualities of some jobs; (ii) an overall training plan for the plant; and (iii) the absenteeism policy.[9]

To many commentators the combination of (1) a 'good' base-line union–management relationship and (2) a management willingness to allow the union to act as a 'partner' in both the design and implementation stages of a human resource management approach will further enhance the quality of the (already good) union–management relationship by ensuring that collective bargaining and HRM have essentially a complementary relationship.[10] However, what factors will encourage management to allow the union to have such a partnership role? The factors that have frequently been mentioned in this regard include the following:

1   the need to respond to some competitive problems in the product market;

2   a relatively highly unionized workforce, and a relatively influential union, which management cannot avoid dealing with as a fact of life; and

3   a relatively positive experience (from both the union and management points of view) with the initial, rather limited, HRM initiatives, which are incrementally developed over the course of time.[11]

It is these and other insights that we will seek to develop at various stages in this book.

This section has very largely drawn on some US experience and literature in order to develop some propositions which, as noted above, we will pursue further. Are there any findings and lessons that we can also draw from national systems of industrial relations other than that of the US? This is the matter we now turn to address.

## INSIGHTS FROM OTHER NATIONAL SYSTEMS

A recent review of industrial relations developments in some seventeen European countries observed the existence of certain common trends in the 1980s.

- employers seeking greater flexibility and decentralization of decision-making;

- weaker union movements, variously involving lower levels of union organization and less inter-union co-operation/co-ordination;

- government initiatives to deregulate the labour market and tighten control of public expenditure;

- a weakening of 'corporatist' (highly centralized, tripartite) industrial relations arrangements; and
- a reduced overall level of strike activity.[12]

The decline of unionization and collective bargaining arrangements was, as was noted in the Introduction, a tendency in the 1980s that was certainly not confined to Britain and the USA. The contents of Table 2.4 provide some relevant information in this regard.

Has HRM played a role in the decline of unionization and collective bargaining in some of these systems? There are certainly suggestions along these lines for some individual systems. For example, Table 2.4 indicates a low and declining rate for unionization in France, and the 'encouragement of worker participation without union involvement' has been noted as an increasingly

Table 2.4   *Changes in union density, various countries, 1980–8*

|                | 1980 | 1988 | 1980–8 |
|----------------|------|------|--------|
| Australia      | 49   | 42   | −7     |
| Austria        | 54   | 46   | −8     |
| Belgium        | 57   | 53   | −4     |
| Canada         | 35   | 35   | 0      |
| Denmark        | 77   | 73   | −4     |
| Finland        | 70   | 71   | 1      |
| France         | 19   | 12   | −7     |
| Germany        | 37   | 34   | −3     |
| Italy          | 49   | 40   | −9     |
| Japan          | 31   | 27   | −4     |
| Netherlands    | 35   | 25   | −10    |
| New Zealand    | 55   | 42   | −13    |
| Norway         | 57   | 57   | 0      |
| Sweden         | 80   | 85   | 5      |
| Switzerland    | 31   | 26   | −5     |
| United Kingdom | 51   | 42   | −9     |
| United States  | 23   | 16   | −7     |

*Source*: Richard B. Freeman and J. Rogers, 'Who speaks for us? Employee representation in a nonunion labor market', in B.E. Kaufman and M.M. Kleiner (eds), *Employee Representation: Alternatives and Future Directions*, Madison, Wisconsin, Industrial Relations Research Association, 1993, p. 16.

common practice there in the 1980s.[13] The general trend towards decentralized management decision-making has also posed some new and potentially awkward questions for unions in relatively centralized industrial relations systems where the level of union organization held up relatively well in the 1980s. In Germany, for instance, the number of organizations with quality circles has grown substantially: from around 30 organizations in the late 1970s to some 1,200–1,400 in the latter part of the 1980s.[14] The growth of quality circles and team working arrangements in Germany in the 1980s initially provoked some concern and opposition among unions and works councils, although from the mid-1980s works-level agreements in the motor and chemical industries have increasingly guaranteed a role for works councils in the establishment and operation of such arrangements.[15] Indeed the unions (and works councils) in Germany appear to have taken a much more pro-active, partnership stance with regard to these HRM practices than is the case with many unions in other systems. Table 2.5 contrasts the stance of IG Metall in Germany with that of a leading Canadian union.

The examples in Table 2.5 would seem to suggest that unions in more centralized industrial relations systems with less of a tradition of adversarial collective bargaining are relatively more capable of adjusting and responding to the introduction of (a relatively homogeneous set of) HRM practices; this interpretation is obviously similar to that of the intra-system perspective of the previous section. An alternative view is that HRM practices themselves are not a homogeneous entity across national industrial relations systems. That is, there may be important differences in (1) the employer motivation for introducing HRM practices, (2) the processes by which the practices are introduced and (3) the content or components of the practices themselves. Such differences are likely to derive, in turn, from historically-based differences in the larger context of the national industrial relations system. This is certainly the view of Brewster and his colleagues, who have argued that (1) HRM practices differ between European countries, although (2) there is a greater difference between Europe (as a whole) and the USA, particularly as regards the role of unions and the extent of government involvement.[16] As a very crude indicator of the position in Europe we have constructed Table 2.6 on the basis of some of the data in the European HRM study conducted by Brewster and his colleagues. The table contains a rank ordering of the countries

Table 2.5   *Union views about HRM: contrasting illustrations*

1   *Canadian Auto Workers Union (CAW) Guidelines on Work Reorganization*

- We reject the use of techniques such as Kaizan (pressure for continuous improvement) where the result is speed up, work intensification and more stressful jobs.
- We oppose workplace changes which limit mobility, weaken transfer rights and erode seniority provisions.
- We reject the introduction of alternative workplace structures and employee-based programmes which purport to represent workers' interests while circumventing the union.
- We reject efforts to shift compensation from wages to incentives and to individualize the rewards of productivity improvements.

2   *The IG Metall Policy Approach to Team Working*

- A broad assignment of varying tasks for the group (including long cycle times).
- Group competence in decision-making in areas such as job rotation, division of the work, quality control and training needs.
- Decentralization of the plant decision-making structure.
- Selection of production organization and technology suitable for group work (based on decentralized technology and production concepts).
- Equal pay for group members.
- Equal opportunity for all, including special training where necessary for the disabled and socially disadvantaged, to participate in group work.
- Support for the personal and occupational development of individuals and the group.
- Regular group meetings, at least one hour per week.
- Representation of group interests within the established plant system of interest representation.
- Voluntary participation in the groups.
- Pilot projects to test the functioning of group work before broader implementation.
- A joint steering committee at the firm level, with equal labour and management representation, to oversee and co-ordinate the implementation of group work and the activities of the group.

*Sources*: *Canadian Auto Workers Union, Statement on the Reorganization of Work*, 1989; L. Turner, *Democracy at Work*, Ithaca, Cornell University Press, 1991, pp. 113–14.

according to (1) the decline of union influence in organizations (as reported by management) and (2) increases in verbal and written communication to employees. The aim was to see whether the countries in the group with the most (least) reported union decline closely coincided with the group with the most (least) communication increases to individual employees; the latter is an important HRM practice in its own right, and may constitute something of a proxy for a more general HRM orientation. Clearly the rankings for the ten countries do not overlap all that closely, casting doubt on any suggestion that union decline is closely associated with the increased use of this particular HRM practice; the most notable exceptions to this general statement are France and the UK, where the rankings are very close.

The results of this 'very crude test' are hardly surprising, as there are few commentators who would be likely to argue that HRM practices have been the sole, or even a major, cause of a decline in union influence in organizations. Rather, the results of this exercise are arguably more useful in suggesting that HRM

Table 2.6  *Reported union decline and communication to employees*

| Country | Decreased union influence | Increased verbal communication to employees | Increased written communication to employees |
|---|---|---|---|
| Switzerland | 5 | 9 | 4 |
| Germany | 7 | 8 | 8 |
| Denmark | 6 | 3 | 6 |
| Spain | 6 | 7 | 8 |
| France | 2 | 3 | 1 |
| Italy | 3 | 4 | 7 |
| Norway | 9 | 6 | 9 |
| Netherlands | 8 | 5 | 5 |
| Sweden | 4 | 1 | 2 |
| UK | 1 | 2 | 3 |

1 = most; 9 = least.
*Source*: C. Brewster, 'European HRM: reflection of, or challenge to, the American concept', in P.S. Kirkbride (ed.), *Human Resource Management in Europe*, London, Routledge, 1994, pp. 65–6.

practices are not a homogeneous entity across national boundaries. That is, the employer motivation for introducing them, and the way they are introduced, are likely to differ according to different national contexts and circumstances.[17] Both historical traditions and current political circumstances are frequently stressed as important sources of differences in this matter.

In US versus European comparisons, reference is frequently made to the historically stronger anti-union traditions of American employers, the traditionally limited role of government intervention in the labour market and the anti-union stances of the Republican administrations of the 1980s. However, differences also exist within Europe. Clearly Britain has diverged from the relatively centralized bargaining arrangements of Europe, and there was little counterpart in Europe to the sort of union legislation passed in Britain in the 1980s. Furthermore, in France and Portugal, employment protection legislation was weakened in the 1980s, whereas in Italy and Spain it was strengthened, and it is quite possible that such differences have importantly shaped how unions view the nature of HRM practices. In short, the generic principle embodied in HRM practices (namely, the tendency to 'individualize' industrial relations) has obviously raised similar concerns and worries for unions across national boundaries. But the extent of these concerns seems to vary considerably, depending on perceptions of employers' motivations in introducing them and the actual processes of their introduction, with these, in turn, deriving from the larger context of the national system: in a system with a strong social partnership tradition, such as Germany, union concerns about HRM practices certainly appear considerably weaker than in systems without such a tradition.

## HRM: SOME ADDITIONAL OBSERVATIONS

The concept and practice of HRM have attracted both strong proponents and strong critics, but with much of the discussion and debate overwhelmingly based on *a priori* arguments, and using only limited empirical evidence based on illustrative examples and selected case study organizations. This state of affairs is both surprising and unsatisfactory, given the very powerful claims for and criticism of HRM, namely that it can (1) positively impact on the level of organizational effectiveness and performance and (2) negatively impact on the level of union organization.

Admittedly there are some empirical studies whose findings are not inconsistent with these alleged effects. In relation to the first effect, some US research has shown that (i) the firms where HRM is more integrated into the process of strategy formation have higher levels of performance;[18] (ii) the export performance of firms is positively related to a comprehensive HRM approach;[19] and (iii) the effective integration of the production and human resource management systems results in positive productivity and product quality differentials for motor vehicle manufacturing plants across a number of countries;[20] in Britain, some research has also shown that some individual HRM practices are positively associated with management perceptions of above-average establishment-level performance.[21] As to the second effect, some US research has indicated that certain HRM practices are associated with maintenance of non-union organizational status over time,[22] while studies in Australia[23] and Ireland[24] have indicated that particular HRM practices are associated with low levels of union organization in individual establishments at a particular point in time. In the latter studies, however, the lack of information on both the date of introduction of such practices and changes in union organization over time means that it is not clear which particular line of causation is involved in this observed relationship.

Obviously the HRM literature needs considerably more comprehensive and systematic studies of these alleged effects before it can reasonably claim to have a strong empirical grounding. This particular limitation of the existing literature has been noted in a number of review articles.[25] There are also some existing criticisms of HRM in practice, as opposed to criticisms of the relevant body of literature, which need to be noted at this stage; these are, however, criticisms of the practice in the USA, which may be less true in other systems. The first of these is the so-called 'integration hypothesis', which contends that too many HRM innovations are viewed and introduced by management as discrete, stand-alone innovations.[26] Instead of this piecemeal, *ad hoc* introduction of individual changes, it is argued that a coherent, mutually reinforcing set of measures needs to be put in place. In short, it is having a (coherent and consistent) package of HRM measures, rather than the individual measures, that is all-important in terms of contributing to enhanced organizational effectiveness. Table 2.7 provides an illustrative example of this line of argument by indicating a set of HRM changes to accompany the operation of a TQM (total quality management) programme.

The second, and more recent, criticism of HRM practice is essentially as follows:

> Human resource management theory has yet to move beyond its individual firm boundaries. This limits its utility as an analytic device in settings where the probability of adopting and sustaining

Table 2.7 *TQM and complementary HRM policy changes*

---

- In selection decisions, the willingness of employees to learn new skills needs to be tested; it is important to identify individuals who can function well in group settings, and a realistic preview of expected behaviours needs to be provided.

- Training programmes must reach beyond specific job skills to cover topics such as team work, time management, decision-making skills, etc.

- Career development must seek to provide employees with a systems orientation, which means that greater emphasis must be placed on cross-functional experience obtained via horizontal (rather than vertical) work assignments and moves.

- The strong individual orientation and emphasis of the performance appraisal process needs to be changed. More emphasis needs to be given to evaluating contributions to team performance, involving peers in the appraisal process, and making the process less competitive between individuals.

- Pay systems centred around individual job descriptions, job worth and individual merit increases are inconsistent with TQM's emphasis on collective responsibility, horizontal relationships and horizontal learning. Instead, skills-based payment systems, profit-sharing or group-based performance pay arrangements are more appropriate.

- Differences in terms and conditions of employment based on hierarchical position need to give way to an all-salaried workforce or single-status arrangements.

- Adversarial, arm's-length collective bargaining needs to be replaced by much more of a joint problem-solving approach.

- Much more emphasis needs to be given to establishing channels of two-way communication concerning strategy and performance.

---

*Source*: Adapted from D.E. Bowen and E.E. Lawler, 'Total quality orientated human resources management', *Organizational Dynamics*, 1992, pp. 34–40.

investments in human resource practices depends on whether other firms in one's product and/or labor markets adopt complementary innovations.[27]

The particular concern being expressed here is that the incentive of any one organization to invest in and maintain a commitment to a particular HRM innovation will be undermined if other organizations do not make a similar commitment. This proposition is frequently illustrated by reference to the particular case of workforce training, with the argument being that employers will only enhance the level of training (with its short-run costs and longer-term benefits) if they can reasonably expect to realize these benefits over time, an expectation that will be undermined by other employers in the industry or local labour market 'poaching' their trained labour. This sort of concern frequently provides the justification for the introduction of a system-wide training tax/levy system.

This second criticism of existing HRM practice in essence contends that an individual organization committed to HRM has a vested interest in having more and more organizations adopt a similar approach. This is an interesting, but potentially very controversial proposition. Firstly, there will be individuals who will question the basic validity of the proposition. For instance, some individuals might want to argue that individual competitive advantage can only arise from 'firm-specific, valuable resources that are difficult to imitate'.[28] If this is the case then individual firms may be extremely reluctant to assist the inter-firm diffusion process. In addition, the proposition implies that the more diffusion the better, a perspective or judgement that has been increasingly questioned by diffusion researchers in recent years.[29] That is, is a widespread diffusion of innovations which may be 'inefficient' for many organizations a 'good thing'? A second possible response is agreement with the proposition, but then the expression of uncertainty or disagreement as to how best to bring about a more widespread diffusion process. For example, some commentators have suggested that HRM innovations (with their short-term costs and longer-term benefits) in a low-labour-cost competitive strategy setting can only be stimulated and diffused by public policy initiatives designed to limit the low-labour-cost option.[30]

For others, however, a more 'positive' public policy may need to be established through acquiring (and building on) more knowledge about the actual processes of HRM diffusion. For instance it has been commented that:

Anecdotal evidence from employers seems to indicate that one of the best ways of predicting whether a high-performance work system will be adopted is for firms to have a model in the same industry. There may be many reasons for this. Behavioural arguments suggest that various kinds of peer pressure and the search for legitimacy at the organizational level generate a need to copy practices of successful firms, whether they are functional or not. Other arguments suggest that because the context in which practices are applied is so critical to their success, it makes sense for management to pursue only practices that can be shown to have succeeded in similar contexts. A related issue, explored in some research on this subject, is that the most important problem when introducing high performance production techniques is not knowledge of the techniques themselves but of how to get them accepted and implemented – issues that may also be specific to context.[31]

The potential importance of the particular industry context in shaping the diffusion process is one of the empirical issues examined in Chapter 5. More generally, the basic position adopted here is that a more widespread diffusion of HRM innovations is desirable, but that the extent of our knowledge as to how this can be brought about is currently rather limited.

## SUMMARY

This chapter has examined the essence of HRM practices and outlined the debate concerning the potential role of such practices in contributing to the decline of collective bargaining arrangements. The central theme of the chapter has been the proposition that HRM will pose much less of a problem for unions in situations characterized by relatively co-operative or joint problem-solving collective bargaining relationships. This would seem to be the case both within and between national systems of industrial relations, and given its potential importance will be returned to at various points in the book.

## REFERENCES

1   *Industrial Relations Review and Report*, 511, May 1992, p. 5.
2   J. Storey, *Developments in the Management of Human Resources*, Oxford, Blackwell, 1992.

3   T.A. Kochan, *Collective Bargaining and Industrial Relations*, Home-wood, Irwin, 1980, pp. 142–50.

4   J.W. Thacker and H. Rosen, 'Dynamics of employee reactance to company and union: dual allegiance revisited and expanded', *Relations Industrielles*, 41 (1), 1986, pp. 128–42.

5   M. Parker and J. Slaughter, 'Managing by stress: the dark side of the team concept', ILR Report, Fall 1988.

6   P. Blyton and P. Turnbull (eds), *Reassessing Human Resource Management*, London, Sage, 1992.

7   *IRS Employment Trends*, 567, September 1994, pp. 2–3.

8   R.E. Walton, 'From control to commitment in the workplace', *Harvard Business Review*, 85 (2), 1985, p. 81.

9   P. Adler, 'The learning bureaucracy: New United Motor Manufacturing Inc.', mimeographed paper, University of Southern California, pp. 78–9.

10  T.A. Kochan, H.C. Katz and R.B. McKersie, *The Transformation of American Industrial Relations*, New York, Basic Books, 1986.

11  Ibid.

12  A. Ferner and R. Hyman (eds), *Industrial Relations in the New Europe*, Oxford, Blackwell, 1992.

13  D. Segrestin, 'Recent changes in France', in G. Baglioni and C. Crouch (eds), *European Industrial Relations*, London, Sage, 1990, pp. 118–23.

14  D. Jacobi and W.M. Jentsch, 'West Germany: continuity and structural change', in Baglioni and Crouch (eds), *European Industrial Relations*, p. 133.

15  D. Jacobi, B. Keller and W.M. Jentsch, 'Germany: codetermining the future', in Ferner and Hyman (eds), *Industrial Relations in the New Europe*, pp. 245–6.

16  See P. Kirkbride (ed.), *Human Resource Management in Europe*, London, Routledge, 1994, chapters 5 and 7.

17  M. Regini, 'Human resource management and industrial relations in European companies', in J.R. Niland, R.D. Lansbury and C. Verevis, *The Future of Industrial Relations*, London, Sage, 1994, pp. 256–69.

18  P. Cappelli and H. Singh, 'Integrating strategic human resources and strategic management', in D. Lewin, O.S. Mitchell and P.D. Sherer (eds), *Research Frontiers in Industrial Relations and Human Resources*, Madison, Industrial Relations Research Association/University of Wisconsin, 1992, p. 170.

19  L.R. Gomez-Mejia, 'The role of human resources strategy in export performance: a longitudinal study', *Strategic Management Journal*, 9, 1988, pp. 493–505.

20  J.P. MacDuffie and T.A. Kochan, 'Does the US underinvest in human resources? Determinants of training in the world auto industry', paper presented at the Academy of Management Meeting, 1991.

21  Employment Policy Institute, 'What has human resource management achieved in the workplace?', *Economic Report*, 8 (3), 1994.

22  J. Fiorito, C. Lowman and F.D. Nelson, 'The impact of human resource policies on union organizing', *Industrial Relations*, 20 (2), 1987, pp. 113–26.

23  R. Harris, 'Variations in union presence and density in Australia: evidence from AWIRS', *Journal of Industrial Relations*, 35 (4) 1993, pp. 571–84.

24  P. Gunnigle, G. McMahon and G. Fitzgerald, *Industrial Relations in Ireland: Theory and Practice*, Dublin, Gill and Macmillan, 1995, Chapter 4.

25  P.B. Beaumont, 'The US human resource management literature: a review', in G. Salaman (ed.), *Human Resource Strategies*, London, Sage, 1992, pp. 20–37.

26  T. Kochan, J.-C. Gershenfeld and J.P. MacDuffie, 'Employee participation, work redesign and new technology: implications for public policy in the 1990s', paper prepared for the Commission on Workforce Quality and Labor Market Efficiency, US Department of Labor, 1989.

27  T.A. Kochan, 'Teaching and building middle range industrial relations theory', in R.J. Adams and N.M. Meltz (eds), *Industrial Relations Theory*, Rutgers, New Jersey, Rutgers University Press, 1993, p. 374.

28  Cappelli and Singh, 'Integrating strategic human resources', p. 186.

29  E. Abrahamson, 'Managerial fads and fashions: the diffusion and rejection of innovations', *Academy of Management Review*, 16, 1991, pp. 586–612.

30  E. Appelbaum and R. Batt, 'Policy levers for high performance production systems', *International Contributions to Labour Studies*, 3, 1993, p. 25.

31  P. Cappelli and N. Rogovsky, 'New work systems and skill requirements', *International Labour Review*, 133 (2), 1994, pp. 217–18.

# 3

# HRM AND THE NON-UNION SECTOR

## INTRODUCTION

Traditionally, industrial relations researchers have had relatively little to say about the non-union employment sector, a sector of employment which is growing in many advanced industrialized economies. In contrast, some commentators have tended, at least initially, to view HRM practices as being of most relevance and applicability in the non-union sector. This perspective undoubtedly stemmed from the fact that many HRM practices were pioneered in certain well-known non-union US firms. Moreover, at least in principle (as we saw in the last chapter) one way in which HRM may have contributed to the decline of collective bargaining is by helping to maintain the non-union status of organizations. That is, such practices may have been important in ensuring a relatively high level of job satisfaction in the non-union sector that has acted to limit the employee demand for union representation and collective bargaining. At the same time, however, some of the evidence briefly mentioned in the introduction suggested that there was relatively little evidence of HRM practices being widely adopted in the non-union sector as a whole in Britain. In view of this fact, which will be further documented here, we instead ask a rather different question, namely, is HRM nevertheless of some significance in particular parts of the non-union sector? This is the theme essentially developed here, with the specific proposition advanced being that HRM practices are likely to be particularly associated with non-union employers who attach a relatively high priority to remaining non-union.

The evidence in support of this proposition constitutes a major part of this chapter; but, before turning to this matter we briefly examine, in turn, the question of the sources of union decline and the position of the non-union sector as a whole.

# THE SOURCES OF UNION DECLINE

As is well known, Britain was one of the leading countries characterized by union decline in the 1980s (see Table 2.5), a process that has continued into the 1990s. The years 1979–90, for instance, saw total union membership decline by more than three million, with the overall level of union density falling by nearly 13 percentage points in these years.[1] The reasons for this decline were initially pursued largely by labour economists whose aggregate level, quantitative analysis variously concentrated on (i) the role of business cycle variables, (ii) changes in the composition of the workforce, and (iii) the influence of government legislation.[2] In practice relatively little agreement has emerged concerning the respective importance of these sets of influences.

More recently, mainstream industrial relations researchers have joined the debate concerning the reasons for union decline in the 1980s and 1990s by emphasizing the potential importance of two other possible contributing factors. The first of these concerns the role of union recruitment and organizing activities, with the major issues raised here being whether individual union recruitment initiatives can raise the overall level of union membership (as opposed to simply redistributing members between unions), and whether such recruitment activities are sufficiently numerous, adequately resourced and focused on the growing areas of the labour market.[3]

The second possible influence concerns the role of increased employer opposition to the presence of unions and collective bargaining arrangements, an influence that has been shown to be particularly important in certain leading US studies in the 1980s.[4] In Britain the issue of employer opposition to collective bargaining has been overwhelmingly pursued through an examination of de-recognition activity whereby management withdraws its voluntary recognition of unions for the purposes of collective bargaining.[5] Currently it is held that de-recognition is rather more common than was initially thought to be the case, is spreading beyond its initial concentration in particular industries (for example provincial newspapers) and is expected to increase in the future.

De-recognition is, however, far from being the only possible manifestation of employer opposition to union representation and collective bargaining. For example, the practice of some multi-

Table 3.1   *Union recognition arrangements at the company level*

| Manual workers | | Non-Manual workers | |
| --- | --- | --- | --- |
| Recognition<br>  of which | 89% | Recognition<br>  of which | 75% |
| All establishments | 50% | All establishments | 32% |
| Some establishments | 33% | Some establishments | 37% |
| No recognition | 11% | No recognition | 25% |

*Source*: P. Marginson et al., *Beyond the Workplace: Managing Industrial Relations in the Multi-Establishment Enterprise*, Oxford, Blackwell, 1988, p. 126.

establishment companies operating their individual establishments on both a union and non-union basis has been noted. Table 3.1 presents some available survey evidence on this matter.

A second company-level survey reported that 'union recognition covering all establishments predominated only amongst the "other" manufacturing sectors, and the four utilities and two financial services companies recognizing unions.'[6] This partial recognition practice can have major implications for the level of union density in large, multi-establishment companies, organizations which play a major role in the British economy.[7] For instance, a study of one such organization revealed the following:

1   In the years 1977–85, total employment in the corporation fell by 46 per cent, with the overall level of union density falling from 65 to 52 per cent. (It is currently below 50 per cent.)

2   This overall change in union density was due to the fact that the highly unionized plants (in mature and declining business areas) were shedding labour in substantial numbers (up to an 80 per cent reduction in some plants), whereas in the non-union plants (in the expanding business areas) employment levels increased by 143 per cent in these years.[8]

There is frequently a perception that the non-union plants in such multi-plant corporations are generally the new or younger ones. Box 3.1 provides an illustrative example along these lines.

Indeed, some recent research has indicated that the probability of new plants recognizing unions for collective bargaining purposes in the 1980s was much less than in previous decades.[9]

Whether this relationship derives from increased management opposition to unions and is associated with the use of HRM practices is examined later in this chapter.

There are some major limitations to the extent of our current knowledge concerning the causes of union decline in Britain. The two most notable ones to be mentioned at this stage are:

1 The various alleged causes of decline have rarely been examined together in individual studies, so that it is not possible to indicate their relative importance in the decline process.

---

### Box 3.1 *A new non-union plant in a multi-establishment company*

This greenfield site involved a joint venture between a British company and two foreign-owned organizations. All the existing plants of the British company are unionized, but the joint venture operation is a non-union one. It was established in the late 1980s, and has some 140 employees, a figure expected to increase to 240 by the early 1990s. The recruitment/selection phase of the operation involved the use of assessment centres and psychometric testing, with the aim being to identify a workforce characterized by 'trainability, flexibility and organizational commitment'; none of the employees selected had a background of experience in the industry concerned. The HRM policy mix of the operation is characterized by (i) harmonization of terms and conditions of employment (as regards length of the working week, pension scheme, sick pay scheme, holiday entitlement and eating facilities); (ii) team-based working operations (the 4 production areas involve individual teams of some 10 employees each) and associated quality circles; (iii) a strong emphasis on direct, two-way communications involving team briefing arrangements and an open-door management approach; (iv) extensive cross-functional training to facilitate functional flexibility, and (v) performance-related pay arrangements. HRM policies along these lines have virtually no counterpart elsewhere in the British company set-up, with the greenfield site establishment being described as their 'state of the art' one in HRM terms.

2   The studies conducted on aggregate-level time-series data are
    not capable of yielding insights into the processes of change
    that are occurring simultaneously (but separately) in the union
    and non-union sectors of employment. For instance, an overall
    fall in union membership and density can variously occur
    through (i) a reduced number of union establishments (for
    example, through closures, de-recognition), (ii) a reduction in
    the average size of union establishments (through, for example
    redundancies), (iii) an increased number of non-union estab-
    lishments, and (iv) an increase in the average size of non-union
    establishments. One suspects that all these factors have been at
    work, but again it is important to have an indication of their
    relative strength.

It is only research conducted at the individual establishment
level that is starting to yield some insights into these separate
processes of change.[10] However, this sort of work clearly needs to
be taken further. One obvious area for further research is to
examine the various factors associated with changing levels of
union density over time at the individual establishment level.
Table 3.2 indicates some of the key findings to emerge from such
an analysis, using the panel data set of the third National
Workplace Industrial Relations Survey.
    The sort of findings reported in Table 3.2 were particularly
important in that changes in manual union density were closely
related to any change in the union or non-union status of
establishments in the period 1984–90. That is, for example, a de-
recognition decision by management very much followed a
sizeable and sustained fall in union density for manual (and non-
manual) employees. This finding clearly suggests that declines in
union density at the level of the individual establishment strongly
shape the *ability* of employers to go non-union through a de-
recognition decision.
    One can arguably generalize from this sort of finding to argue that
the ability of employers to adopt a non-union employment strategy
(be it a de-recognition decision or the opening of a new, non-union
plant) will be very much a function of 'appropriate timing', in the
sense of being concentrated in circumstances and time periods
where union membership and density is declining. For instance, it
is not hard to find plants established in the late 1970s and early
1980s with single recognition arrangements which concede that they
would have gone non-union if they were setting up now. But what

Table 3.2   *The factors associated with changing (manual worker) union density at the establishment level, 1984–90*

---

- Decreases in union density were associated with larger-sized companies.
- Increases in density levels were associated with manufacturing sector establishments.
- Establishments that were part of organizations moving towards multi-establishment status were associated with declining density levels.
- Increases in manual employment were associated with increased density, while increases in the proportion of temporary workers were associated with falling density levels.
- Establishments characterized by relatively sizeable employee share-ownership and extensive consultation over changes in working practices saw increases in density levels.
- Establishments with relatively poor financial performance were associated with declining density levels.
- Establishments operating in international product markets and with increased levels of competition experienced declines in union density.
- Establishments where employee–management relations were deemed (by management) to have deteriorated in the period 1984–90 saw increasing density levels.
- Density levels rose in establishments with less sophisticated production technologies, and declined in establishments that moved towards micro-electronics based technologies.

---

*Source*: P.B. Beaumont and R.I.D. Harris, 'Union de-recognition in Britain: the larger context', *Industrial and Labor Relations Review*, 48 (3), 1995.

about the *incentive* to adopt a non-union employment strategy? This is one of the key questions addressed in the next section.

## THE NON-UNION SECTOR AS A WHOLE

As was argued earlier, industrial relations academics have only very recently begun to examine the non-union employment sector. Much of this early-stage work has been concerned to identify the characteristics of non-union establishments as against ones that recognize unions for collective bargaining purposes.[11] This sort of research has typically revealed that non-union establishments are relatively small-sized, younger-aged, service-sector-based ones in the southern regions of the country, which are less likely to be part of a large multi-establishment organization. More recently, however, attention has been turned to the following questions:

1   What factors provide the incentive (as opposed to ability) of employers to adopt a non-union employment strategy?
2   Are HRM practices an important part of the employment strategy that they have adopted in order to maintain their non-union status?

It is these questions that will be discussed here. In order to discuss the first question it must be recognized that the notion of a 'non-union employment strategy' can involve a relatively diverse, mixed set of activities. For instance there may be very different incentives involved in the following sorts of non-union employment activities:

- the de-recognition of a bargaining unit in a unionized establishment;
- the building of a new non-union plant in a multi-establishment organization where the other plants recognize unions;
- the acquisition of an already existing non-union establishment; and
- the opening of a small, single independent establishment on a non-union basis.

This being said, there are at least two preliminary hypotheses that may be advanced concerning the incentive of organizations to adopt a non-union employment strategy:

1   the role of product market influences, in particular increased competition, the movement into new business activities and changes in the nature of competitive strategy; and
2   previous management experiences or views concerning union representation and collective bargaining arrangements.

Box 3.2 provides an illustrative example of a non-union employment move very much influenced by product market factors.

In this particular case what drove the movement to a non-union plant in the 1990s was (1) the company's movement into a new product market area or business activity and (2) the fact that the

## Box 3.2   *Movement to non-union status: an example*

- This US-owned organization has 7 major production units in the UK, employing some 2,800 people.

- Its corporate-wide HRM philosophy emphasizes employee empowerment, team work, trust and single status.

- In none of its production units are unions recognized for collective bargaining purposes for staff employees.

- It has three basic business divisions, with its oldest plant being established in the 1950s and its newest one in the 1990s.

- The terms and conditions of employment in all plants are among the best in their local labour market areas.

- If one distinguishes between its older plants (1950s and 1970s), 1980s plants and 1990s plant, then one finds the following pattern of developments:

### 1   *The 1950s and 1970s plants*

These two plants currently have about 600 employees each, although they have been shedding labour in recent years. In each plant some three unions are recognized for collective bargaining purposes, with union density on the shopfloor being virtually 100 per cent. In the late 1980s a move to single-table bargaining arrangements was negotiated in one of these plants, while in the early 1990s single-table arrangements were imposed by management in the other plants. These single-table bargaining arrangements have been followed by a rationalization of the shop steward systems, with individual team leaders increasingly substituting for the role of shop stewards and regional union officials rarely being involved in plant-level deliberations.

### 2   *The 1980s plants*

These four plants have between 80 and 150 employees, with employment levels having been relatively stable. All plants have single recognition arrangements with a union not represented in the old plants. Team working arrangements, performance-related pay and pay-for-knowledge schemes, and extensive cross-functional training programmes are widespread.

Box 3.2 *continued*

> Union density on the shop floor is essentially universal, although there are reportedly few members willing to act as shop stewards and the full-time officials rarely visit the plants.
>
> ### 3    *The 1990s plant*
>
> This plant, which was established in the early 1990s, has some 700 employees, a figure that is expected to increase substantially over time. It is a non-union operation, which management see as 'the way forward in the future'. Psychometric testing was used to recruit all employees, it has the most comprehensive single-status terms and conditions package of all the plants, and team working arrangements, although these are not the 'leaderless' teams of the 1980s plants.

major competitor in this new area was a well-known (and highly respected) non-union organization. The importance of product market conditions (particularly difficulties) in shaping a 'union-avoidance' strategy has been shown in some survey research in the US,[12] although work along such lines in Britain is characterized by its essential absence. This being said, it is worth noting that research has shown, firstly, that declines in union density that were the background to a de-recognition decision were associated with increasing levels of product market competition and competition in international markets (Table 3.2), and, secondly, that partial, as opposed to full, recognition arrangements (Table 3.1) were associated with multi-establishment companies characterized by a sizeable range of business activities.[13] The role of product market influences in shaping non-union organizations' views on union organization is considered in the next section.

The second hypothesis to be advanced concerns the *prior* experiences and views of management concerning unions and collective bargaining. Some existing research has shown that senior management in new, small, single independent establishments attached a relatively high priority to being non-union if they had an immediate employment background in a non-union organization.[14] That is, they favoured non-union status for their own organization because of their positive feelings about their prior employment experience in a non-union organization. However, Box 3.3 indicates exactly the opposite sort of relationship. In

## Box 3.3   *A route to non-union status: two cases*

1   This US-owned organization has two plants in Britain. The older plant (established in the 1970s) recognized a union for collective bargaining purposes. The second plant was established in a different part of the country in the early 1980s, has a workforce (mainly women) of some 800 and has remained non-union from its inception. The union that is recognized for collective bargaining purposes in the original plant tried to organize the new one in both 1984 and 1986. However, on both occasions a ballot of the hourly paid employees failed to produce a majority in favour of union recognition. In 1988 the union again attempted to organize the new plant. But on this occasion management refused to agree to a workforce ballot on the issue. At the same time management increased basic pay and holiday entitlement, improved the terms of the sick pay scheme, and introduced a discretionary bonus payment (based on the plant's trading results) and a new grievance procedure. The improved terms and conditions package was 'completely conditional on it being accepted by you as an individual and as being your confirmation that you do not require third party representation'. The strong and growing management opposition to union recognition in the new plant stemmed from the poor union–management relationship in the older plant ('a militant union') and pressure from corporate headquarters, which was taken by local management to imply that union recognition would not augur well for future investment in the plant.

2   In 1979 this plant in the engineering industry had some 2,200 employees. It was a highly unionized plant (approximately 100 per cent organization among both shop-floor and staff employees), with 6 unions being recognized for collective bargaining purposes, and 54 shop stewards and 7 senior shop stewards. In that year the present Managing Director, who openly admits to being unsympathetic to unions, was appointed, with a remit of reversing the heavy operating losses of the plant. In tackling this task he attached a major priority to bringing about industrial relations change, as he was 'horrified' at the extent of overmanning, restrictive working practices, and the power of the unions, which meant that 'everything had to

Box 3.3 *continued*

be negotiated with them'. The years 1979–94 have seen major industrial relations changes in the plant. The workforce has been substantially reduced to a current figure of 730, union membership has fallen to 86 per cent on the shopfloor and 49 per cent among staff employees, there are no senior shop stewards, and only 6 shop stewards in total, the 'last in, first out' basis of redundancy decisions has been removed, and the scope of collective bargaining has been restricted to wages and conditions matters only, with all other items being the subject of information or consultation only. These changes were associated with a number of disputes and strikes throughout the 1980s. In the late 1980s the plant was acquired by another company, which gave strong backing to the approach of the Managing Director, but at the same time placed a 'tough set' of business performance objectives on him for the plant. The result was a list of major changes in working practices which were presented to the workforce; the quid pro quo for agreeing to these changes was a company commitment to invest £10 million in the plant over a five-year period, which was estimated to result in the creation of 350 new jobs.

The proposed changes in working practices were discussed with national union officials and approved in principle, subject to certain modifications and qualifications. However, the shop stewards opposed them, and they were rejected in a workforce ballot (70 per cent vs 30 per cent against change). Following this rejection the company actively began to explore a number of alternative sites for the location of the new investment. The result was the establishment of a greenfield site less than 100 miles from the old plant, which was to be operated on a non-union basis. The non-union plant has been in operation for some 2 years and currently has a workforce of 375 employees. The flexible working practices, which were rejected by the workforce in the old plant, have been in place in the non-union plant from its inception, and single-status terms and conditions are operative there, though not in the older plant. A new HRM manager, who previously worked for a well-known non-union company, was appointed exclusively for the new plant, although all other senior managers are responsible for both the new and the older plants.

these two cases management have set up new non-union plants essentially as an 'adverse' reaction and response to their experience of problems and difficulties with unions in the older plants.

These two hypotheses may not capture the full set of incentives for employers to adopt a non-union employment strategy, although arguably they can constitute a useful starting-point for a rather more developed body of research into this particular subject area.

What is the role of HRM practices in a non-union employment strategy? Is there any evidence that they are being extensively adopted as a 'union substitution device' in the growing non-union employment sector? As was suggested in the Introduction, the answer provided by the evidence of the third National Workplace Industrial Relations Survey is very much a NO to this question. In essence the survey painted the following picture of the non-union employment sector, compared to the union one:

- Employee relations were perceived by management as relatively better in the non-union sector.
- Labour turnover was relatively high in the non-union sector.
- Dismissal rates were relatively high in the non-union sector.
- Workforce reductions were more likely to involve compulsory redundancies in the non-union sector.
- Discipline, grievance and health and safety procedures were less common in the non-union sector.
- Employee consultation and information-sharing was less common in the non-union sector.[15]

As a specific illustration of the lesser presence of formal, institutional arrangements in the non-union sector one can take the case of joint consultative committees, which historically have been viewed as something of an 'integrative bargaining' mechanism. The relevant information is set out in Table 3.3. The table clearly indicates that joint consultative committees have suffered an overall decline in the years 1984–90, although in both those years they were relatively less common in the non-union sector.

The relative absence of HRM practices in the non-union sector as a whole should occasion relatively little surprise. This is because, firstly, non-union establishments are, as we saw earlier,

Table 3.3    *Joint consultative committees, union and non-union establishments, 1984 and 1990 (per cent)*

|                             | 1984 | 1990 |
|-----------------------------|------|------|
| Union establishments        | 41   | 37   |
| Non-union establishments    | 21   | 19   |
| All establishments          | 34   | 29   |

*Source*: D. Metcalf, 'Transformation of British industrial relations? Institutions, conduct and outcomes 1980–1990', Centre for Economic Performance, LSE, Discussion Paper 141, 1993, p. 9.

on average relatively more likely to be smaller-sized establishments that are not part of large, multi-establishment organizations. As a consequence, they are less likely to have either the incentive or the resources to introduce a comprehensive set of HRM practices. Secondly, it has been long recognized that the non-union employment sector is a relatively heterogeneous one, characterized by a great deal of diversity and variation in its employee relations arrangements and practices.[16] Box 3.4 provides an illustration of such diversity.

The task undertaken in the next section is to recognize the existence of such diversity, and then to partition the sector as a whole according to a particular criterion and see whether this partitioning is systematically associated with the presence of HRM practices. However, before turning to this task it is obviously important to ask the question: how is the non-union employment sector *as a whole* managing to maintain itself, and indeed grow, in the relative absence of HRM practices? In other words, if HRM practices are not being extensively used as a union substitution device, how are non-union organizations keeping the unions and collective bargaining arrangements at bay? After all, the non-union employment sector is not without its difficulties; Digital Equipment (a well-known non-union organization), for example, have announced that some 6,000 jobs will go in their European operations in the next twelve months (*Financial Times*, 7 March 1994). The answer would appear to be that (1) relatively limited attempts have been made to organize the non-union sector, owing to factors such as the low visibility of many (small) non-union establishments and the severely limited organizing resources of the unions (in the face of declining membership, finances and other pressing priorities in a high-unemployment environment) and (2) where organizing attempts have been made, they have encountered employer opposition and/or employee indifference.

These propositions receive support from a number of sources:

1 A number of surveys of non-union establishments have indicated that in a relatively high proportion of cases no

---

**Box 3.4  *Employee involvement in Health and Safety: some non-union cases***

1 This organization manufactures industrial ceramics, largely for the steel-making industry. It is a family-owned firm, established 10 years ago, and has some 140 employees. A health and safety committee has existed for 4 years. It consists of 6 shop-floor employees, and the works administrator, and meets on a monthly basis. The shopfloor employees were picked and asked to serve on this committee by the works administrator, and none of them have received any health and safety training.

2 This foreign-owned subsidiary in the electronics industry was established in the mid-1960s and has some 1,600 employees on site. There is a central safety committee for the organization as a whole, separate committees for the 3 divisions of the organization, and individual safety groups operating on the shop floor. The 15 safety representatives, who are elected by the workforce, have been extensively trained and are represented on all committees and groups. This particular organization has been the recipient of numerous health and safety awards.

3 This foreign owned organization is in the electronics industry, was established in the mid-1970s and has some 600 employees. A works committee, which meets on a monthly basis and has 10 elected workforce representatives, has a broad-ranging remit, including health and safety. In addition, team briefing arrangements provide health and safety information to employees on the shop floor.

*Source*: P.B. Beaumont 'Select committee', *Occupational Safety and Health*, February 1993, pp. 29–33.

---

attempt has been made to recruit members and obtain recognition there.[17]

2   A recent survey of small non-union employers in the service sector revealed that the majority would oppose a recognition attempt, or thought it unlikely to occur.[18] Furthermore, the vast majority of employees in this study indicated the absence of an interest in joining a union if the opportunity arose.

3   The number of recognition claims brought to ACAS (admittedly not a comprehensive or necessarily representative indicator of all union organizing activity) has actually fallen over time (as the non-union sector has grown), from 329 (1980) to 122 (1992). Moreover the union 'win rate' (that is, full or partial recognition achieved) has fallen from nearly 1 in 2 claims in the late 1970s to around 1 in 5 at the present time.

A number of these issues will be returned to in later chapters.

## DIVERSITY AND HRM PRACTICES WITHIN THE NON-UNION SECTOR

The sort of variation apparent in Box 3.4 has been captured to a considerable extent in the relatively long-standing distinction drawn between better standards (that is, union substitutionists) and lower standards (that is, union suppressionists) non-union employers.[19] The former are organizations that provide above-average terms and conditions of employment and utilize a range of progressive HRM policies (for example, extensive employee involvement and communications arrangements) to try to minimize employee job dissatisfaction, and hence any employee demand for union representation. In contrast, the latter organizations are characterized by relatively lower terms and conditions of employment and a limited (some would say non-existent) range of HRM policies, and instead rely largely on their small size (and hence limited visibility and appeal to unions) and recruitment/dismissal practices to avoid a union presence.

There have been a number of more recent attempts to refine and develop this basic dichotomy of non-union organizations.[20] These attempts all involve essentially two common themes, namely to identify (1) the varying extent of management concern about and opposition to a possible union presence and (2) the particular means (strategy/tactics) that management adopt to implement their varying concern about the opposition to a possible union role. This body of literature has been overwhelmingly based on case studies of individual organizations, which obviously raises questions about the extent to which one can generalize about the categories identified. However, this literature does yield the central proposition to be examined here, namely that those non-union organizations that attach a relatively high priority to union avoidance will be the ones most likely to make use of HRM practices.

Fortunately, some information contained in the third National Workplace Industrial Relations Survey allows us to examine this particular proposition.[21] In essence the survey revealed that approximately 1 in 3 non-union establishments were relatively strongly opposed to the notion of a union presence, with the remaining two-thirds expressing much more neutral attitudes. This finding, firstly, raises the question of why this particular sub-group attaches a relatively high priority to the avoidance of unions.

One possible explanation is that these particular non-union establishments are relatively similar in terms of their organizational and workforce characteristics to the establishments that unions have traditionally concentrated their organizing activities on. And, as a consequence, the management in these non-union organizations have a particular concern about becoming a union organizing target. An analysis of the data revealed considerable support for this particular proposition. Specifically we found that:

1 Those non-union establishments that were most opposed to a possible union presence were relatively larger-sized, older-aged establishments in the manufacturing sector, and were located in the northern part of the country. That is, they had similar characteristics to traditional union-organized establishments.

2 The management belief that they would constitute a relatively attractive organizing target for unions clearly had some basis in reality. This was because a significantly larger proportion of the non-union establishments most opposed to a possible union presence had, when compared with the neutral non-union group, experienced a union recruitment attempt in the years 1984–90.

A second reason why this particular sub-group of non-union employers might attach a relatively high priority to union avoidance is the management belief that the establishment is performing relatively well, but that a union presence would impede such performance. Again, some analysis of the survey data provided some support for this proposition, in that:

1   The non-union establishments most opposed to a possible union presence had higher perceived levels of labour productivity than those non-union establishments less opposed to a union presence.

2   The panel data in the survey also revealed that the non-union establishments that were most opposed to a union presence had in the years 1984–90 grown faster and were more likely to report an improved employee–management relationship than the non-union establishments that were much more neutral concerning a possible union role.

Finally, at this stage, it is important to note that the non-union establishments most opposed to a possible union presence were situated in much more competitive product market settings. This particular relationship is clearly highly consistent with the previous section's discussion of the importance of product market factors in shaping a non-union employment strategy.

If these are the factors or considerations that help account for their relatively strong opposition to a possible union presence, how have they sought to avoid unions in practice? Specifically, what is the evidence that they have made some use of HRM practices for this purpose? The analysis of the survey data again yielded some useful findings that seemed to point in the HRM direction: (1) quality circles and employee share-ownership schemes were significantly more likely to be associated with the non-union establishments most opposed to a possible union presence; and (2) the dismissal rates of these particular non-union establishments were significantly lower than for non-union establishments that were more neutral in attitude. Box 3.5 provides an illustrative example of the type of non-union organization discussed above.

## THE PARTICULAR CASE OF NEW PLANTS

A number of the illustrative examples provided in this chapter (Boxes 3.1–3.3) concern relatively newly-established non-union plants. More importantly, a number of survey-based studies have documented a relatively strong relationship between non-union status and younger-aged plants.[22] The most important evidence to this effect comes from a recent publication by Millward, which revealed:[23]

1   Only 29 per cent of workplaces established since 1984 recognized unions, compared with 40 per cent of all workplaces in 1990.

2   This age effect or relationship has become more pronounced over time; in 1980 the incidence of recognition among establishments less than 10 years old was 45 per cent, whereas in 1990 the corresponding figure was 24 per cent.

---

**Box 3.5   *A priority attached to avoiding unions:  an example***

This US-owned corporation has production plants in a number of countries, all of which are non-union ones. In order to help maintain its (world-wide) non-union policy, corporate management regularly conducts employee attitude surveys in all plants; such surveys were conducted, for instance, in 1991, 1992 and 1994. The survey findings for each plant are then compared with the corporate average for that year, and with earlier years' results for the individual plant concerned. Following the report of the survey's findings, a management problem-solving taskforce is established in each plant (with a corporate-level taskforce acting as a co-ordinating device) to address the major problem areas identified by the survey. The problem areas are defined as ones where employees attach a relatively high level of importance to the issue, but are relatively dissatisfied with the issue or subject concerned. The 1994 survey findings for the British plant indicate that the management problem-solving task will (until the next survey) need to accord particular attention to bringing about changes in the following areas:  performance appraisal;  career development;  and communication. For instance, the levels of employee dissatisfaction in the British plant (compared to the corporate average) were 29 per cent (16 per cent) in relation to employee empowerment, and 36 per cent (21 per cent) in relation to communication.

---

3   The drop in the rate of recognition among newer workplaces was particularly marked in the manufacturing sector.
4   New establishments were created at a relatively fast rate in the 1980s, which, with their lower rate of recognition, accentuated the decline in the overall extent of recognition.

What underlies the strong relationship between non-union status and newer workplaces? Is it essentially due to (1) strong management opposition to unions allied with the extensive use of HRM practices or (2) low establishment visibility and limited union organizing resources and attempts? To some extent both sets of factors will be at work, given that new plants can variously involve:

- small single independent establishments;
- new plants established by (domestic) multi-establishment organizations; and
- foreign inward investors.

In short, the population of new workplaces is far from being homogeneous in nature. However, it would appear on balance that the extensive use of HRM practices (as a union substitution device) has provided only a relatively limited part of the answer. The various measures of HRM practices examined by Millward were not disproportionately concentrated in the newer, non-union establishments.[24] Rather the predominant characteristics of the newer workplaces provide some potentially useful pointers concerning the factors involved in their non-union status. In essence the new workplaces generally (compared to the population of workplaces):[25]

- were smaller-sized, service-sector establishments;
- had relatively few skilled manual workers, and more part-time, women workers;
- were branches of larger enterprises; and
- frequently involved relatively short-distance changes of site.

In short, these characteristics on balance would seem to point to the importance of low visibility and limited union recruitment activity as a major explanation of their non-union status. This is not to discount totally the role of employer opposition to a union presence; but clearly the sort of 'sophisticated' opposition (allied with HRM practices) discussed in the previous section is unlikely to be the main explanation for the population of new non-union workplaces.

To date we have in this chapter concentrated very largely on non-union employers. But what about employees in the non-union sector? How do they feel about their employment circumstances? The importance of addressing this particular question follows from an earlier finding reported in this chapter, namely that institutional arrangements for information-sharing, consultation and grievance-handling are relatively under-developed in the non-union sector. This finding from the third National Workplace Industrial Relations Survey would appear to provide a strong *a priori* case on equity grounds for eliminating the institutional vacuum in the British industrial relations system. But to investigate this case more fully it is obviously important to examine the views of the non-union workforce concerning this matter.

## THE VIEWS OF THE NON-UNION WORKFORCE

The data examined in this section are concerned with the levels of job satisfaction of non-union employees compared to union employees. These data are designed to shed some light on two particular questions:

1.  Is there any evidence that non-union employees are concerned about the relative absence of institutional arrangements for meeting their on-the-job needs for information, consultation and grievance processing?
2.  Is there evidence of a demand for union representation, which is grounded in concern and dissatisfaction with their jobs?

The data presented here come from some specially requested tabulations of the British Social Attitudes Survey. This survey, which involves an annual, national probability sample (some 1,700 respondents prior to 1986 and since then some 3,000), aims to monitor public attitudes to a wide variety of social, economic, political and moral issues during the 1980s and 1990s. The data presented here come from respondents in employment (between 830 individuals in 1985 and 1,432 individuals in 1989) and indicate their responses to three leading questions asked about the nature their responses to three leading questions asked about the nature of their working environment, namely their views of the quality of employee–management relations, how well the workplace is managed, and whether they want more say in decisions concerning their jobs. These specially requested tabulations compare the responses of non-union and union employees to these three questions for four separate (annual) surveys; this is certainly the largest and most representative set of information concerning this issue. The basic results are set out in Table 3.4.

From Table 3.4, it is apparent that in all four years non-union employees report better perceived employee–management relations and better managed workplaces than their union counterparts, and at the same time are seeking less say in their jobs than is the case with union workers. Do these findings undermine the case for seeking to remove the institutional vacuum in the British industrial relations system? In other words, why should 'outsiders' worry about the existence of an institutional vacuum if the workers concerned apparently do not? One possible explanation of the findings is that a well-informed workforce has 'self-selected' to work in the non-union sector in the full knowledge of the limited institutional arrangements for meeting employee information, consultation and due process needs there.

In fact, however, the reality of the Table 3.4 findings is arguably more subtle and complex than any interpretation such as the above. The first point to note here is the one made earlier on the basis of the third National Workplace Industrial Relations Survey findings, namely the relatively high dismissal and quit rates in the non-union sector. This relatively heavy use of 'exit' mechanisms in the non-union sector is hardly consistent with the 'self-selection' argument that employees have willingly entered the non-union sector in the full knowledge of the limited institutional arrangements for meeting their on-the-job needs for information, consultation, etc. The second issue involved in interpreting the findings of Table 3.4 has to do with the level and nature of employee *expectations*. And there are arguably two separate dimensions to this notion. The first has to do with the very fact of union membership itself, which tends to raise employee knowledge (and hence expectations) of the relative terms and conditions of their jobs. As one American authority has put it:

> One of the by-products of union [voice] is the politicization of the firm's workforce, and union members can be expected to express

Table 3.4   Aspects of reported job satisfaction, non-union and union employees, selected years

| Questions | 1985 | | 1987 | | 1989 | | 1993 | |
|---|---|---|---|---|---|---|---|---|
| | Non-union | Union | Non-union | Union | Non-union | Union | Non-union | Union |
| 1 Quality of employee–management relations[a] | 87.1 | 77.9 | 86.4 | 76.4 | 85.7 | 71.8 | 81.2 | 75.6 |
| 2 Management of workplace[b] | 85.0 | 76.5 | 85.5 | 72.0 | 83.0 | 75.2 | 83.1 | 70.5 |
| 3 Should have more say in decisions affecting jobs[c] | 28.5 | 43.2 | 35.5 | 59.3 | 34.8 | 57.4 | 43.9 | 63.7 |

[a] Percentage answering 'very good', and 'quite good'.
[b] Percentage answering 'very' and 'quite well' managed.
[c] Percentage answering 'should have more say'.

Source: P.B. Beaumont and R.I.D. Harris, 'The institutional vacuum in British industrial relations', Policy Studies, 15 (Winter), 1994.

less job satisfaction than non-union workers. That is, the exit–voice model states that in order for firms to hear the workers effectively, the firm's workforce must express itself 'loudly'. Note, however, that this dissatisfaction is not genuine in the sense that it leads to quits, but is instead a device through which the union can tell the firm that its workers are unhappy and are demanding more.[26]

The strength of the union as a voice mechanism in this regard is such that union workers have been found to report relatively lower levels of job satisfaction in surveys conducted in various countries;[27] at the same time, however, they have relatively low quit rates.

A second possible reason for expecting lower levels of expectation among non-union workers (and hence the findings of Table 3.4) has to do with the characteristics and composition of the workforce in this particular sector of employment. It has, for instance, been argued that the employee decision to work in the non-union sector is a 'highly constrained choice', in that the limited skills, experience, marketability, etc. of the workforce give them relatively limited labour market opportunities and alternatives.[28] This contention is consistent with union relative wage studies, which have invariably argued that the 'human capital content' of the non-union workforce is less than that of the unionized workforce, although it is important to emphasize that this point has only been made in relation to *manual* employees. If there is something to this line of argument we should observe some noticeable differences in the composition of the (manual) workforce in the non-union and union sectors. Table 3.5 provides some support for this particular argument, with the non-union sector having a relatively high proportion of part-time workers, women workers, secondary workers and less skilled manual workers.

Given the interpretation offered of the Table 3.4 findings we do not think that they seriously undermine the equity argument in favour of eliminating the institutional vacuum in the British industrial relations system. At the same time, however, these findings do not obviously constitute 'good news' for a union movement that has overwhelmingly relied on establishing adversarial collective bargaining relationships as a result of a sizeable presence of employee job dissatisfaction. This possible implication of the findings is returned to in later parts of the book. Interestingly, a recent US study reported a considerable latent demand

Table 3.5   *Composition of the workforce, union and non-union sectors (private sector only), 1990*

|  | Non-union sector | Union sector |
|---|---|---|
| **% of total workforce** | | |
| Part-time[a] | 21.05 | 13.26 |
| Manual[a] | 59.26 | 66.49 |
| Women[a] | 41.99 | 30.43 |
| Outworkers | 1.28 | 0.56 |
| Freelancers[a] | 4.32 | 1.52 |
| Temporary workers | 0.95 | 0.98 |
| **% of workforce by occupational group** | | |
| Managers[a] | 7.63 | 6.16 |
| Senior professional/technical[a] | 6.23 | 3.73 |
| Junior professional/technical[a] | 7.14 | 4.61 |
| Supervisors[a] | 3.98 | 5.01 |
| Clerical[a] | 15.88 | 13.78 |
| Skilled manual[a] | 18.71 | 24.71 |
| Semi-skilled manual[a] | 16.70 | 19.97 |
| Unskilled manual | 23.41 | 21.12 |

[a] Mean difference significant (5% level).

*Source*: P.B. Beaumont and R.I.D. Harris, 'The institutional vacuum in British industrial relations', *Policy Studies*, 15, Winter 1994.

for some form of collective, institutional representation among non-union employees, but not one involving traditional, adversarial collective bargaining arrangements.[29] It is important for further research to see if a similar demand is present in Britain.

## SUMMARY

This chapter has been concerned with the employment strategies and practices of the non-union employment sector in Britain. The main general point made is that the non-union employment sector has been growing, but that this growth has not been associated with the extensive introduction and use of HRM practices. However, we have been able to move beyond this very general statement to highlight a number of more specific points which include the following:

- Non-union status is strongly and increasingly associated with younger-aged workplaces.
- Non-union establishments that attach a relatively high priority to union avoidance do utilize certain HRM practices.
- For many non-union establishments their low visibility combined with severe limitations on union organizing activities helps to maintain their non-union status.
- Employees in non-union establishments appear to have relatively high levels of job satisfaction, which does not obviously augur well for traditional union recruitment approaches.

## REFERENCES

1   D. Metcalf, 'Transformation of British industrial relations? Institutions, conduct and outcomes 1980–1990', Centre for Economic Performance, LSE, Discussion Paper 151, 1993.
2   See, for example, A. Carruth and R. Disney, 'Where have two million trade union members gone?', *Economica*, 55, 1988, pp. 1–19; R. Freeman and J. Pelletier, 'The impact of industrial relations legislation on British union density', *British Journal of Industrial Relations*, 28 (2) July, 1990.
3   P.B. Beaumont and R.I.D. Harris, 'Union recruitment and organizing attempts in Britain in the 1980s', *Industrial Relations Journal*, 21 (4), 1990, pp. 274–86; R. Mason and P. Bain, 'The determinants of trade union membership in Britain: a survey of the literature', *Industrial and Labor Relations Review*, 46, 1993 pp. 332–51.
4   R.B. Freeman and J.L. Medoff, *What Do Unions Do?* New York, Basic Books 1984; T.A. Kochan, H.C. Katz and R.B. McKersie, *The Transformation of American Industrial Relations*, New York, Basic Books, 1986.
5   T. Claydown, 'Union derecognition in Britain in the 1980s', *British Journal of Industrial Relations*, 27 (2) 1989, pp. 214–25.
6   P. Marginson, P. Armstrong, P. Edwards and J. Purcell with N. Hubbard, 'The control of industrial relations in large companies: an initial analysis of the second company level Industrial Relations Survey', Warwick Papers in Industrial Relations 45, 1993, pp. 55–6.
7   J. Purcell, 'The impact of corporate strategy on human resource management', in J. Storey (ed.), *New Perspectives on Human Resource Management*. London, Routledge, 1989, pp. 67–91.

8    P.B. Beaumont, 'Industrial restructuring and union density: The experience in one large corporation', *Employee Relations*, 9, 1987, pp. 14–16.

9    R. Disney, A. Gosling and S. Machin, 'What has happened to union recognition in Britain?', Centre for Economic Performance, LSE, Discussion Paper 130, 1993.

10   P.B. Beaumont and R.I.D. Harris, 'Trade union recognition and employment contraction: Britain 1980–84', *British Journal of Industrial Relations*, 29, 1991.

11   P.B. Beaumont and R.I.D. Harris, 'The north–south divide in Britain: the case of trade union recognition', *Oxford Bulletin of Economics and Statistics*, 51, 1989, pp. 413–28.

12   W.N. Cooke, *Labor–Management Co-operation*, Kalamazoo, Michigan, Upjohn Institute for Employment Research, 1990.

13   P. Marginson, P.K. Edwards, R. Martin, J. Purcell and K. Sisson, *Beyond the Workplace: Managing Industrial Relations in the Multi-Establishment Enterprise*, Oxford, Blackwell, 1988, p. 128.

14   P.B. Beaumont and I. Rennie, 'Organisational culture and non-union status of small businesses', *Industrial Relations Journal*, 17 (3), 1986, pp. 214–24.

15   N. Millward, M. Stevens, D. Smart and W.R. Hawes, *Workplace Industrial Relations in Transition*, Aldershot, Dartmouth, 1992, pp. 363–5.

16   P.B. Beaumont, *The Decline of Trade Union Organization*, London, Croom Helm, 1987.

17   TUC, *Organising for the 1990s*, London, TUC, 1989, p. 26.

18   *IRS Employment Trends*, 538, June 1993.

19   Beaumont, 'Industrial restructuring'.

20   I. Beardswell, 'Management style and non-union employers', paper given at the Employee Relations Conference, Cardiff Business School, September 1993.

21   P.B. Beaumont and R.I.D. Harris, 'Opposition to unions in the non-union sector in Britain', *International Journal of Human Resource Management*, 5, 1994.

22   Beaumont and Harris, 'The north–south divide'. See also Disney, Gosling and Machin, 'What has happened to union recognition?'

23   N. Millward, *The New Industrial Relations?* London, Policy Studies Institute, 21, 1994, pp. 28–9.

24   Ibid., Chapter 5.

25   Ibid., p. 120.

26   G. Borjas, 'Job satisfaction, wages and unions', *Journal of Human Resources*, 14 (1), 1979, p. 25.

27  Freeman and Medoff, *What Do Unions Do?*, pp. 136–49.
28  P. Blyton and P. Turnbull, *The Dynamics of Employee Relations*, London, Macmillan, 1994, pp. 243–4.
29  R.B. Freeman and J. Rogers, 'Who speaks for us? Employee representation in a non-union labor market', in B.E. Kaufman and M.M. Kleiner (eds), *Employee Representation: Alternatives and Future Directions*, IRRA Research Volume, Wisconsin, Madison, IRRA, 1993, pp. 28–34.

# 4

# HRM AND THE UNION SECTOR

## INTRODUCTION

As we saw in Chapter 2, HRM was initially seen by many academics and practitioners as essentially an 'individualized approach' to industrial relations (concentrating on individual employees rather than unions), which was pioneered in the non-union sector of the United States. Given the essence and origins of these practices, considerable attention was initially given in the US to the question of how unions would react, respond and adjust to them. The national union leadership in the US (at least at the level of the AFL–CIO) has provided only limited clear-cut guidance to the lower levels of the union movement concerning such practices,[1] although it is now clear that a great deal of activity has been occurring 'on the ground'. This is because some evidence currently suggests that HRM practices have spread more widely in the union than in the non-union sector of employment.[2]

As a consequence of the above evidence it is now being increasingly argued that HRM practices are not inherently anti-union devices, and that HRM and collective bargaining should not be viewed as discrete, mutually exclusive sets of practices or arrangements. Indeed some commentators have even gone further, in arguing that a union presence is not necessarily a constraint on the spread of HRM practices, but may, at least in certain circumstances, be a positive asset in the processes of adopting and maintaining such practices over time.[3]

This evolution of the debate concerning HRM practices and unions in the US is, at least to some extent, being paralleled in Britain. That is, the initial debate in Britain about whether HRM practices will spread at all[4] has moved on to a new stage, where the question being asked is more that of why these practices are relatively more prevalent in the union sector of employment?[5] It is important to note that some of the more high-profile introductions of HRM practices have occurred in union firms in other countries. In France, for instance, considerable attention was focused on the consultation agreements of Thompson CSF in 1989 and Renault in 1990.

It is the evolution of these themes that is explored in this particular chapter. However, before presenting our British material concerning these matters, we begin by looking at the US position in a little more detail.

## THE MESSAGE FROM AMERICA

As HRM practices originated in the non-union employment sector, it was hardly surprising that US unions were initially sceptical, not to say critical, of them; indeed such views still remain within individual parts of the trade union movement.

Initially, there was some variation in union attitudes towards HRM practices, both within and between individual unions, depending on factors such as (1) varying assumptions concerning product demand/technological developments and (2) different ideological premisses.[6] However, the predominant union position was for long one of 'decentralized neutrality', with the national union leadership basically leaving it up to each local branch as to how it should respond to any employer-initiated HRM approach.[7] The national unions did, however, invariably urge the locals to seek 'certain protections' if they were to become involved in such programmes. The sort of protections which were sought in practice have been classified into two broad groupings:[8]

1   direct control over outcomes, involving negotiated provisions that limited or specified certain outcomes (for example no redundancies, the sharing of financial gains); and
2   indirect influence over the process (for example provisions providing for union participation in the planning/design stages, a role in the choice of consultants, restrictions on the range of subjects to be discussed).

In short, in the absence of a more pro-active stance from the national union leadership, one observed an essentially reactive stance from unions at the local level, with the major concern being to ensure that HRM practices did not cut into the traditional subject-matter of collective bargaining. More recently, there are signs of a more pro-active stance being adopted at the national union level. This is not so much associated with the union confederation (the AFL–CIO), but rather with some individual national unions, such as the steelworkers and communication workers. And the prime reason for this change is simply a recognition of the realities of organizational life, namely that employer HRM initiatives are increasingly going to occur, with or without the blessing of the unions. Indeed, as we noted above, there is now some evidence to indicate that (1) HRM practices are more widespread in the union than in the non-union sector and (2) the maintenance of such practices over time seems to be assisted by a union presence.[9]

The increasing spread of HRM practices within the union sector in the US raises at least two important questions for consideration:

- What are the processes by which HRM has spread in union-ized plants?
- What are some of the leading lessons for unions involved in these processes of change?

The US literature seems to suggest that HRM practices have been introduced in unionized establishments via two very different routes.[10]

1 Management has essentially imposed these HRM practices via a hard bargaining approach, deriving from a combination of pressing product market circumstances and difficulties and problems in the existing union–management relationship; *or*

2 management has conceded a 'partnership' role to the union where the level of union membership is relatively high, and 'good' (prior) union–management relationships exist. In these particular circumstances the initial introduction of a limited range of HRM practices has frequently been developed and expanded incrementally over the course of time.

For unions one of the major lessons to be learned regarding the operation of HRM practices has been to do with managing the 'internal politics' of the process, at least where a 'partnership' role

is involved. The major problem for the unions in the partnership route to change is that political opposition within the union
will almost inevitably emerge, alleging that the local union leadership has 'sold out' to management. In order to try to head off,
or deal with, such internal opposition, local unions closely
involved in the operation of extensive HRM programmes have
had to pay increasing attention to extending and improving
communication with their rank-and-file membership. Table
4.1 indicates the various steps that the local union (UAW) has
taken in this regard in the Saturn case, which is the leading
example of union–management co-operation in the US at the
present time.

In summary, American experience to date reveals essentially the
following picture:

1  The national union leadership has been relatively slow to take
   a pro-active position in relation to HRM practices.
2  HRM practices are now relatively more prevalent in the union
   sector of employment.
3  HRM practices have been introduced by management via
   either a hard bargaining or a union partnership route.
4  The union partnership route requires the unions to manage the
   politics of the change process carefully, particularly by improving their communication with the rank-and-file membership.
   The unions have also had to make other internal changes and
   adjustments, such as devolving their levels of decision-making
   and providing more training to union representatives concerning the nature and implications of HRM practices.

In the remainder of this chapter we consider the extent to which
experience and practice in Britain reveals a similar, or a divergent
story.


## UNIONS AND HRM PRACTICES IN BRITAIN

The contents of Table 4.2 capture well some of the early concerns
and reservations of many unions in Britain concerning HRM
practices. This relatively critical and reactive approach essentially
embodied the following elements:

1   HRM practices are an attempt by management to individualize industrial relations, and, as such, have the potential to undermine, or at least conflict with, union organization and collective bargaining arrangements.

Table 4.1   *Inter-union communication at Saturn*

---

- *Congress*: twice-a-month meetings attended by all local union executive board members, union module advisers, crew co-ordinators, and other key staff functional co-ordinators. The purpose of the congress is to provide the local union with strategic direction and focus on specific issues.

- *Leadership Team*: approximately 50 top union leaders, including elected officers, executive board members, and crew co-ordinators. It meets every week and conducts periodic workshops to discuss the partnership, union strategy and business issues.

- *Work Unit Counsellors*: bi-monthly meetings are held between elected union officers and elected work unit counsellors to discuss their roles and responsibilities as both production team leaders and elected union representatives.

- *Block Meetings*: weekly meetings between module advisers, work unit counsellors, and crew co-ordinators to provide communications and discuss operating problems and issues in each module.

- *Rap Sessions*: monthly meetings held in each Business Team between the local union president and union members in an open question-and-answer forum.

- *Town Hall*: monthly local union meetings held twice during the normal work day to facilitate the participation by crews on both first and second shifts.

- *Member-to-Member Surveys*: annual surveys utilizing the team leaders to conduct formal 45-minute interviews with every individual union member (5,300 in 1992) on the issues, concerns or needs they would like to see addressed by the union. The 1991 member-to-member survey served as the basis for the union's negotiating platform in the contract renewal process that year.

---

*Source*: S. Rubinstein, M. Bennett and T. Kochan, 'The Saturn Partnership: co-management and the reinvention of the local union', in B.E. Kaufman and M.M. Kleiner (eds), *Employee Representation: Alternatives and Future Directions*, Madison, Wisconsin, Industrial Relations Research Association, 1993, p. 358.

2   However, product market and labour market pressures and circumstances are such that some employers will undoubtedly seek to introduce such practices.

3   The case for union involvement (or not) must be made at the level of the individual workplace, depending on the particular circumstances of each case.

4   Any such involvement must, however, be conditional upon the local union's obtaining certain safeguards, concessions and quid pro quos; in particular, the prime role of collective bargaining must be maintained.[11]

In short, we have an early-stage response very similar to that observed in the USA. Is there any sign of the nature of this response having changed over the course of time? One recent

Table 4.2 *ASTMS (as it then was) on quality circles*

---

- Quality circles only extend worker participation on management's terms.

- As an alternative channel of workforce–management communication, quality circles can undermine the position of supervisors and challenge existing collective bargaining arrangements.

- In comparison to collective bargaining, quality circles have a number of disadvantages, namely that members are self-appointed or selected by management, discussion is restricted to the immediate work area, management retains the right to accept, reject or amend proposed solutions and they promote a 'false identification' with management aims.

- However, as individual employees appear to gain some personal satisfaction from quality circle involvement, their possibilities should not be rejected out of hand. But management's motives for introducing them should be fully examined and the union needs to be in a strong enough position to have the circles operating in a context where there is an expansion of collective bargaining.

- In situations where quality circles cannot be resisted, there need to be safeguards and quid pro quos, including the provision of extensive company information, regular updates on the savings generated through the circles and union input into the selection of circle volunteers.

---

Source: *Industrial Relations Review and Report*, 385, 1987.

review claimed to have detected something of a change, citing in support of this judgement the following evidence:

- national union and TUC-level statements emphasizing the need for individual organizations increasingly to adopt product quality and innovation-based competitive strategies, with a consequent need to attach increased priority to workforce training, career development, etc., matters; and
- increased instances of unions in individual organizations moving away from a position of boycotting or ignoring certain HRM developments, and instead seeking to 'engage positively' and shape such developments.[12]

In contrast, one leading union official in Britain (John Edmonds, General Secretary of the GMB) has characterized the British union response to HRM as 'incoherent, tentative, anxious, befuddled and uncertain'.[13] Nevertheless signs of change are apparent in individual unions in Britain, changes frequently driven by the need to catch up with the reality of workplace-level practice. For example, the 1991 Biannual Delegate Conference of the TGWU voted to move away from their position of principled opposition to HRM practices.[14] In 1993 the GMB issued an important brochure on HRM. It was sceptical of the motives of some managements in introducing such practices, and raised some concerns about the implications of such practices for unions and collective bargaining. At the same time, however, it recognized the inevitability of changes along these lines, and acknowledged that they might produce some benefits for members and that local officers and members needed more information and guidance concerning an appropriate response. The latter concern was reflected in the issuing of briefing notes for team working, annualized hours, performance-related pay, job evaluation, profit-sharing and profit-related schemes, and total quality management. The general guidelines contained in the document are set out in Table 4.3.

More recently, the General Secretary of the TUC has gone on record as follows:

We do not fear the agenda of the human resource development manager. We prefer a people-orientated system to a money-orientated one with the accountant in the driving seat – as is the case in far too many British companies. I believe that unions can have their own distinctive agenda with the human resource development company; it is not a traditional agenda but lies, for example, in the areas of ensuring that training is linkable to external qualifications, of ensuring that women at work receive special attention, of reducing working time, of pointing up single-status issues, of keeping an eye on executive pay (which has reached obscene levels in some cases) and of raising questions about pay systems, management styles, and future plans. In all these, there is a rich and fertile territory for the creative union.[15]

This statement is of particular significance in view of the recent reorganization and relaunch of the TUC. As part of this exercise a task group was established to develop 'trade union responses to the human resource management agenda'. The task force report, which was presented to Congress in 1994, essentially made the following points:

1   The rhetoric of HRM frequently exceeds the reality of HRM, with such practices being adopted in an *ad hoc*, piecemeal

Table 4.3 *GMB guidelines on HRM*

---

- It is important to identify new management techniques as early as possible and to try to secure implementation only on the basis of agreement. However, it may not be possible to prevent implementation, in which case securing benefits from the change will be important.

- Remember that these techniques may be seen as positive by members, especially if they offer a bigger say in decision-making, better training and an end to repetitive work.

- Do not allow the trade union role to degenerate into a token one. Argue for an increase in union representation and try to keep it as near the shop floor as possible. Be positive about the trade union agenda – better training, flexibility to suit workers, job security.

- Watch out for developments that enhance the role of supervisors or team leaders and/or attempt to undermine the collective identity of workers. This may involve keeping a close eye on the employers' wider objectives – especially attempts to persuade workers to identify their interests solely in terms of the company's.

- Keep the membership informed at all times. Advise them of the dangers, particularly to the role of the union and the local representative; but discuss with them any areas of potential benefit.

---

Source: *GMB, HRM/TQM*, London, GMB, 1993, p. 10.

fashion, and in some cases being a 'smokescreen' for anti-union initiatives.

2  Individual elements of HRM are more a feature of union, than of non-union workplaces.

3  A high-quality competitive strategy, involving minimum labour standards, long-term continuing training and an end to the short termism of capital markets is favoured.

4  Organizational change is inevitable, and should be handled through a joint partnership route.

5  This joint partnership route should place considerable emphasis on employment security and a widened collective bargaining agenda. Training, health and safety, and equal opportunities should be major new elements in this agenda.

6  The collective bargaining process needs to become less adversarial in nature, which will require changes from both management and unions.

7  Full-time officer briefings and shop steward training needs to be increasingly provided, to convey more information about HRM.

In short, the initial approach of ignoring HRM, condemning it as an across-the-board principle, or leaving local representatives to work out their own solutions has given way to more of an emphasis on the processes of introduction and the resulting internal (union) adjustments which are necessary. The reasons for this change are well captured in the observations of Bill Jordan of the AEEU:

Whether we like it or not, these practices amount to a modern industrial development that is here to stay. It must be our job to ensure that they are introduced in a way that is of maximum benefit to our membership. A refusal to acknowledge HRM would give the opponents of social partnership an opportunity to cast the trade union movement as negative and as being stuck in the past. Frankly, in my view, there would be some justification to this charge. Our adoption of an oppositionalist line would also deny us the opportunity to differentiate between good and bad management. At present AEEU support for HRM in its form at Toyota, Nissan and Sony allows us to be critical of those companies that try to use these techniques as a cloak for attacks on their workforces. In reality, companies will introduce these techniques regardless of our opposition. Let us not leave our shop stewards with the unenviable task of trying to respond to change with no guidance or practical support from their union or from the wider trade union movement.[16]

In short, the basic message above was that the unions needed to change their response to HRM in order to catch up with the realities of change in the workplace. It is to these realities that we now turn.

## HRM AND THE UNION SECTOR

In the last chapter we observed that joint consultative committees were more a feature of the union than of the non-union employment sector. But given the relatively long history of joint consultative committees in Britain, this finding could, at least at first glance, be dismissed as saying relatively little about the adoption of new HRM practices in the union sector. However, this would not in fact appear to be the case, as collective bargaining arrangements seem not only to be associated with joint consultation, but also with relatively more in the way of new HRM practices. For example, a survey of company-level employment practices in the late 1980s reported that:

> Quality circles also appeared to be strongly related to the presence of trade unions. None of the companies which did not recognise trade unions reported having quality circles. Furthermore, they were also more likely where four or more of the methods of communication we specified were used and where there was joint consultation. In short, quality circles appear to be part of a wider strategy for winning the hearts and minds in highly unionised workplaces.[17]

In fact, further analysis of this particular data set suggested 'that to the extent that there is a human resource management policy in British industry' two variants of the approach were apparent: (1) joint consultation, task participation (quality circles) and two-way communication in the union sector and (2) financial participation (profit-sharing) in the non-union sector.[18] The relatively greater presence of employee-involvement practices in unionized establishments has also been documented in some smaller, less representative surveys.[19]

However, what does our largest, most representative and up-to-date data set, namely the third National Workplace Industrial

Relations Survey, reveal? As Sisson has noted, this survey does not fully address all the HRM-related issues and practices that one would ideally like to have information on (for example, manpower planning, appraisal arrangements, training and development);[20] hence his suggestions for some new questions in a future survey. This being said, it is clear that the information contained in the 1990 survey points to the relatively greater presence of HRM practices in the union sector. For example, the key basic findings concerning newly-introduced arrangements for employee involvement were as follows:

1   48 per cent of establishments had recently introduced new arrangements according to the 1990 survey, compared to 35 per cent in the 1984 one; and

2   within the private sector in 1990, initiatives were reported in 48 per cent of union establishments compared to 36 per cent of non-union ones; this differential remained when controlling for similar-sized establishments.[21]

Are findings of this kind 'good news' for the unions? In one sense they very much are. This is because the relatively greater presence of HRM practices in the union sector demonstrates that there is no inherent incompatibility between HRM practices and union representation and collective bargaining. The demonstration of this fact is important in indicating that an employer who is strongly committed to introducing HRM practices does not necessarily have first to remove any existing collective bargaining arrangements. In Box 4.1 we provide two illustrative examples of the introduction of HRM practices in unionized establishments.

However, beyond this very general, but not unimportant statement, some important issues, not to say problems, may still confront the unions. Such issues are likely to derive from the fact that the (management) motives for, and the processes of, introducing HRM practices may vary considerably; the relative absence of clear-cut national union guidelines concerning an appropriate response will not have helped in this regard. For instance, one recent survey of 62 organizations reported that some 80 per cent of these recognized unions, with around half of these saying that the unions had been receptive to the employee-involvement initiatives introduced;[22] in some 20 per cent of the union organizations management acknowledged that the employee-involvement initiatives were designed to weaken the union role. A recent

**Box 4.1   *HRM in a unionized environment: two cases***

1 This pharmaceutical manufacturing plant has some 270 employees and recognizes three unions for collective bargaining purposes, with union density on the shopfloor being nearly 100 per cent. In the late 1980s the plant faced the very real possibility of closure. This was because of duplication of product lines and over-capacity in the larger group of which it was a part, and the plant's 'poor reputation' within the group as a whole on the costs, customer satisfaction and industrial relations fronts. In 1989 the newly appointed plant director launched a major programme of organizational change, which, among other things, sought to reduce the number of individual job classifications on the shop floor, initiated a major programme of cross-functional training, incorporated responsibility for quality into the job descriptions of operators and removed all levels of supervision. This programme of change was extensively discussed in the long-standing works committee, which includes representatives of all the unions. Following these deliberations, the plant director initiated a set of group discussions with the workforce as a whole. A joint working party was established to work out the details of the multi-skilling programme and a system of team briefing arrangements was established to inform employees of the stages of development. The programme has been on-going over a three-year period that has seen the subsequent emergence of autonomous work groups on the shop floor. Dismissals and redundancies have occurred in these years.

2 This foreign-owned plant in the chemical industry was established in the late 1950s. It currently has 743 employees, is highly unionized (100 per cent on the shop floor), with five unions being recognized for collective bargaining purposes. The overall union(s)–management relationship is described as 'a good, constructive one', with the plant being characterized by a strong historical commitment to communication, workforce training and health and safety improvement. In the early 1990s a divisionalization move within the larger corporation greatly enhanced the level of operating autonomy of the plant; some older product lines closed, but new ones were brought in. The plant launched a major programme of organizational

Box 4.1 *continued*

change which included (1) moves towards single-status terms
and conditions (for example, elimination of clocking-in; introduction of monthly pay); (2) the introduction of five-shift,
annual hours working arrangements; (3) changed working
practices (for example, changed roles of supervisors/charge-
hands; introduction of analytical trouble-shooting teams); and
(4) new communications arrangements (for example, employee
attitude surveys; senior management briefings of the workforce
four times per year). In order to ensure that they 'carried the
unions with them' in this change process, management took
various steps. Firstly, they ensured that all existing communications arrangements with the unions remained in place, with no
changes in the composition of the committees or the frequency
with which they met. Secondly, all shop stewards and full-time
officials were extensively involved in the early-stage discussions of the overall change programme. Indeed, the initial
presentation to the workforce as a whole was done jointly.
Thirdly, the working parties that oversee the individual elements of the change programme include union representatives.
For instance, the working party on the five-shift/annual system
involved nine individuals, seven of whom were union representatives. This particular working party produced a range of
optional arrangements that were then put to a workforce
ballot.

internal document concerning Cadbury suggests that management is proposing to weaken the union role by increasingly
concentrating consultation and communication arrangements
directly on individual employees (*Financial Times*, 24 November
1994). Such findings point up the need for trade unions and
researchers to move away from highly general statements about
HRM and to examine the following sorts of matters more
closely:

- What were the differing motives (and hoped-for effects) of
  management in introducing HRM practices?
- Were such practices concentrated in establishments with relatively adversarial, or co-operative, union–management
  relationships?

- Were the practices essentially imposed on the unions via hard bargaining, or did the unions play more of a partnership role?
- What safeguards did the union seek for their involvement in the introduction of such practices?
- Have any union–management conflicts arisen, and how have they been resolved?
- What have been the implications for existing collective bargaining relationships?

An important start in examining the sort of questions listed earlier has been made by Storey.[23] Some of the leading findings to emerge from his research are as follows:

1  Established collective bargaining arrangements and new HRM practices tended to constitute dual, parallel arrangements.
2  The above in considerable measure reflect the fact that different groups of management were responsible for the established and the new practices.
3  Conflictual, rather than harmonious, industrial relations characterized the organizations concerned.
4  A tougher, more assertive management stance towards unions was apparent, which sought to reduce (rather than replace) their role.
5  The process of collective bargaining was being decentralized.
6  The unions were not centrally involved in the processes of change (nor indeed was the personnel management function); the bargaining for change (joint partnership route) was the exception, rather than the rule.
7  Union representation and collective bargaining were less of a management priority than previously.
8  The union representatives were generally suspicious of the new HRM techniques.

For the unions the most positive finding to emerge from Storey's work was the essential absence of de-recognition moves, and indeed the limited development of any comprehensive plan to marginalize the unions. However, the much less positive ones were that some more *ad hoc* moves had reduced their role, and certainly they were not centrally involved in the processes of change.

## SOME ADDITIONAL EVIDENCE

If one combines the findings of the Workplace Industrial Relations Survey with those of Storey, then two basic questions arise: why are HRM practices relatively more prevalent in the union sector? And why have such practices rarely been introduced via a joint partnership approach (which has lessened the management priority attached to collective bargaining)? These two questions are closely related, and in order to try to answer them one can initially consider two very different perspectives on the change process in the industrial relations sphere of activity:

1 A problem-based view of the change process, where the emphasis is on management's *incentives* to change in order to overcome existing industrial relations problems and difficulties; this view is unlikely to favour the joint partnership approach, as management is reacting adversely to the existing relationship.

2 An emphasis on the *ability* to change, where a good existing industrial relationship provides a natural basis for the relatively smooth introduction of new practices; this view is more consistent with the partnership route being adopted, as here management is endorsing and seeking to build on the existing good-quality relationship.

These differing perspectives were examined by using the Workplace Industrial Relations Survey to construct an index of HRM practices.[24] The index consisted of the following elements:

- establishments where management provide a good deal of information to the workforce concerning performance;
- establishments with any change in employee involvement in the last three years;
- establishments with changes in working practices that have reduced job demarcation in the last three years;
- establishments with a new consultative committee and/or more meetings concerning participation/communication in the last three years; and

- establishments with autonomous work groups and/or re-organization of work and/or increased responsibility given to employees and/or quality circles and/or training or briefing groups introduced in the last three years.

The use of cluster analysis identified four major clusters, with some two-thirds of the private sector establishments being in the non-HRM cluster. The size of this group is obviously highly consistent with the general view that the diffusion of HRM practices throughout the British system of industrial relations has been relatively limited to date. The next step in the analysis was to see whether there was any relationship between the HRM practices index (the non-HRM group versus the other three clusters) and personnel managers' assessment and rating of the overall employee–management relationship in the establishment; in the latter case we distinguished between a 'very good' rating and the rest.

The basic findings for the union sector are set out in Table 4.4. The pattern revealed in the table certainly seems more consistent with the incentive, rather than the ability, to change emphasis outlined earlier. When both the union and non-union sectors were included in the analysis, it was found that there was a significant three-way interaction effect between (1) the index; (2) the assessments of employee–management relationships; and (3) union/non-union status. More specifically, it was found that HRM

Table 4.4 *Percentage of unionized establishments introducing HRM by 1990*

|  | State of management–employee relations | | | | |
|---|---|---|---|---|---|
|  | Very good | Good | Quite good | Average | Bad |
| % where HRM introduced | 36.3 | 41.5 | 42.0 | 44.4 | 42.8 |

*Source*: P.B. Beaumont and R.I.D. Harris, 'Good industrial relations, joint problem solving and HRM: issues and implications', paper presented at the International Industrial Relations Association Meeting, Washington DC, 1995.

practices in the union (non-union) sector were associated with poorer (better) employee–management relationships.

In summary, it would appear that union establishments seem to have introduced HRM to try and improve the state of existing employee–management relations (that is, an incentive effect), whereas in the non-union sector the introduction of HRM practices has been facilitated by the (relatively good) state of existing employee–management relationships (that is, it is an ability effect) and can be viewed as an initiative to ensure the continued maintenance of such relationships.

These results have offered some explanation of why HRM practices are currently more prevalent in the union than the non-union sector in Britain, and why such practices in the union sector have rarely been introduced via the joint partnership route – that is, there is more pressure/incentive for change as a result of dissatisfaction with the existing relationship in the union sector. Moreover, these results do not appear to constitute 'good news' for a union movement that views HRM and collective bargaining as complementary in nature, and favours the former's introduction via a joint partnership route that would obviously involve an expanded agenda for collective bargaining.

## SUMMARY

In this chapter the concentration has been on HRM practices and the union sector. Specifically, we have observed considerable parallels between the British and American experience in the sense of HRM practices becoming increasingly a feature of the union, rather than non-union, employment sector, and with national union policy concerning HRM practices seeking increasingly to adjust to this organizational reality. With HRM being more a feature of the union, rather than the non-union, sector, many union officers would undoubtedly like to see a pattern of adoption whereby HRM practices were introduced and developed incrementally over time as a result of (i) relatively co-operative union–management relationships; (ii) a joint partnership approach to the change programme; and (iii) initial positive experience (from both parties' points of view) with the early-stage practices. This is not, however, the reality in the union sector at the present time in Britain. As a consequence it is highly questionable to assume that the relatively high incidence of HRM practices in the union sector means that the unions have provided an important input to the processes of introducing such practices.

## REFERENCES

1   T.A. Kochan and K.R. Wever, 'American unions and the future of worker representation', in G. Strauss, D.G. Gallacher and J. Fiorito (eds), *The State of the Unions*, IRRA Research Volume, Madison, Wisconsin, IRRA, 1991, p. 377.

2   A.E. Eaton and P.B. Voos, 'Unions and contemporary innovations in work organization, compensation and employee participation', in L. Mishel and P.B. Voos (eds), *Unions and Economic Competitiveness*, Armonk, New York, Sharpe, 1992, pp. 173–215.

3   See the new preface in T.A. Kochan, H.C. Katz and R.B. McKersie, *The Transformation of American Industrial Relations*, Ithaca, New York, Cornell University Press, 1993.

4   J. Storey and K. Sisson, 'Limits to transformation: human resource management in the British context', *Industrial Relations Journal*, 20, 1989.

5   K. Sisson, 'In Search of HRM', *British Journal of Industrial Relations*, 31 (2), 1993, pp. 201–10.

6   H.C. Katz, 'The debate over the reorganization of work and industrial relations within the North American labor movements', mimeographed paper, ILR School, Cornell University, 1986.

7   T.A. Kochan, H.C. Katz and N. Mower, *Worker Participation and American Unions: Threat or Opportunity*, Kalamazoo, Michigan, Upjohn Institute for Employment Research, 1984, Chapter 6.

8   A.E. Eaton, 'The extent and determinants of local union control of participation programs', *Industrial and Labor Relations Review*, 43 (5), 1990, pp. 604–21.

9   R. Drago, 'Quality circle survival: an explanatory analysis', *Industrial Relations*, 27, 1988.

10   T.A. Kochan and J.C. Gershenfeld, 'Innovation or confrontation: alternative directions for American industrial relations', in W.-C. Huang (ed.), *Organized Labor at the Crossroads*, Kalamazoo, Michigan, Upjohn Institute for Employment Research, 1981, pp. 27–62.

11   P.B. Beaumont, 'Trade unions and HRM', *Industrial Relations Journal*, 22 (4), 1991, pp. 300–8.

12   *Industrial Relations Review and Report*, 511, May 1992.

13   Cited in *IRS Employment Trends*, 552, January 1994.

14  M.M. Lucio and S. Weston, 'Human resource management and trade union responses: bringing the politics of the workplace back into the debate', in P. Blyton and P. Turnbull (eds), *Reassessing Human Resource Management*, London, Sage, 1992, pp. 223–9.

15  J. Monks, 'A trade union view of WIRS 3', *British Journal of Industrial Relations*, 31 (2), 1993, p. 233.

16  Cited in R. Taylor, *The Future of the Trade Unions*, London, Deutsch, 1994, p. 120.

17  P. Marginson, P.K. Edwards, R. Martin, J. Purcell and K. Sisson, *Beyond the Workplace: Managing Industrial Relations in the Multi-Establishment Enterprise*, Oxford, Blackwell, 1988, p. 111.

18  Ibid., p. 121.

19  S. Milner and E. Richards, 'Determinants of union recognition and employee involvement: evidence from London Docklands', *British Journal of Industrial Relations*, 29 (3), 1991, pp. 377–90.

20  Sisson, 'In search of HRM', p. 209.

21  N. Millward, M. Stevens, D. Smart and W.R. Hawes, *Workplace Industrial Relations in Transition*, Aldershot, Dartmouth, 1992, pp. 175–80.

22  *IRS Employment Trends*, 545, October 1993.

23  J. Storey, *Developments in the Management of Human Resources*, Oxford, Blackwell, 1992, Chapter 9.

24  P.B. Beaumont and R.I.D. Harris, 'Good industrial relations, joint problem solving and HRM: issues and implications', paper presented at the International Industrial Relations Association Meeting, Washington DC, 1995.

# 5

# THE INSTITUTIONAL VACUUM AND THE ISSUE OF DIFFUSION

## INTRODUCTION

The starting-point for this book has been the observation that although traditional collective bargaining is declining, there is little sign of an alternative set of institutional arrangements emerging in the growing non-union employment sector. This raises two questions for consideration, namely: does the existence of such an institutional vacuum matter, and how might one try to fill it? These questions largely shape the subject-matter of this particular chapter.

In the first section some analysis and evidence is presented that suggests that the vacuum does matter, in the sense that it would appear to be associated with certain dysfunctional effects and implications that should be of concern to practitioners and policy-makers.

Following this we then turn to look at some of the historical 'challenges' to collective bargaining, which were briefly mentioned in Chapter 1. These were employee-relations initiatives, prior to the rise of HRM practices in the 1980s, which sought to complement, rather than replace, the role of collective bargaining. The prime purpose of looking at this historical experience is to identify some of the leading constraints on the diffusion of employee-relations innovations, which will have to be increasingly addressed in the near future if the existing institutional vacuum is to be closed.

Finally we look at the role of some existing instruments of public policy that have sought to reduce the existing constraints on diffusion, with a view to highlighting their strengths and limitations as regards the present institutional vacuum in the non-union sector.

## DOES THE INSTITUTIONAL VACUUM MATTER?

There are many commentators who would answer yes to the above question, although the reasons given for this answer may well take a number of different forms. Firstly, some individuals will largely concentrate on the declining role of collective bargaining, with particular concern being expressed about the loss of the voice/institutional response face of unionism (see Chapter 1). For example, some commentators have expressed concern about a declining union role in 'pushing' management to introduce positive organizational changes such as an enhanced level of workforce training,[1] while others have demonstrated that this declining role has been associated with a rise in earnings inequality.[2] A second centre of concern about the institutional vacuum is likely to focus more on the position of employees in the non-union sector. And here the concern is essentially that the inadequate spread of HRM practices (as an alternative to collective bargaining) means that the consultation, information-sharing and due process needs of the non-union workforce are being inadequately met. This particular argument is one that was examined and discussed at some length in the final section of Chapter 3.

One possible response to such concerns would be to argue that these are an unfortunate, but inevitable cost of a government policy that has produced a more efficiently functioning labour market, which, in turn, has enhanced the greater competitive performance of the British economy. In other words, that enhanced efficiency and competitiveness have come at the expense of equity, but that this is a cost well worth paying.

In order to examine this argument one needs to distinguish the two leading (but interrelated) dimensions of present government labour market policy. The first is the Government's strong (arguably enhanced) commitment to the relatively long-standing low-labour-cost competitive strategy of the British economy, and the second is the new 'de-regulation' dimension of policy since 1979, namely the sizeable package of labour market reforms that have sought to reduce union power, enhance the rewards of work relative to unemployment/non-work related benefits, reduce government/institutional influence on market outcomes, expand self-employment, etc. Table 5.1 indicates that the low-labour-cost position of Britain is far from being a recent phenomenon.

What does the available evidence have to say about the effectiveness and success of these two dimensions of policy? The low-labour-cost competitive strategy has come in for a great deal of critical comment from industrial relations academics.[3] The major points made in this regard are that such a competitive strategy has: (1) been a major source of the adversarial union–management relationships (distributive bargaining) that have traditionally characterized British industrial relations; and (2) limited the priority that management attaches to employee–management considerations in strategic decision-making processes. The latter has meant, for instance, that personnel management specialists have traditionally had limited representation at the board level, and that industrial relations or HRM decisions are rarely viewed by senior management as strategic decisions.[4] More generally, there are larger concerns about the effectiveness of the low-cost competitive strategy. Michael Porter, for example, has noted that 'analysis of changes in world export share between 1978 and 1985 contains grounds for concern about

Table 5.1    *Labour costs in manufacturing, OECD countries, 1964–74: total hourly labour costs including social charges (GB = 100)*

| Country | 1964 | 1970 | 1974 |
|---|---|---|---|
| Belgium | 105 | 124 | 175 |
| Denmark | 119 | 141 | 188 |
| France | 103 | 103 | 118 |
| Germany | 119 | 145 | 185 |
| Great Britain | 100 | 100 | 100 |
| Italy | 93 | 111 | 122 |
| Netherlands | 95 | 126 | 184 |
| Austria | 80 | 92 | 120 |
| Finland | 102 | 94 | 126 |
| Norway | 122 | 148 | 189 |
| Sweden | 153 | 179 | 208 |
| Switzerland | 110 | 118 | 157 |
| Canada | 192 | 207 | 186 |
| USA | 268 | 253 | 194 |
| Japan | 42 | 66 | 105 |

Source: G.F. Ray, 'Labour costs in OECD countries, 1964–1975', *National Institute Economic Review*, 78, 1976, p. 58.

the path of development of the economy. Far more competitive industries in Britain have lost world export share than have gained it.'[5] Other studies have noted that it is only in industries characterized by low research intensity and where price is an important determinant of competitiveness that British firms have been relatively successful in international markets.[6]

If the low-cost competitive strategy has not served Britain particularly well to date, there are even greater doubts concerning its strength in the future. To many strategy theorists non-price sources of competitive advantage (such as R&D expenditure, workforce training, etc.) will be of increased significance and importance to advanced industrialized economies in the future.[7] And here it is apparent that Britain is in a relatively disadvantageous position.

For example, a study by the Department of Trade and Industry reported that listed British companies increased R&D expenditure by 9 per cent in 1993, a rate of increase greater than that of the UK's main international competitors. However, it was aptly noted that:

> The UK has far to go, however, before it even comes close to matching other countries in its spending on R&D in relation to sales, profits or dividends. The international top 200 companies as a whole devoted on average 4.85 per cent of 1993 turnover to R&D, compared with 2.29 per cent for the 13 British companies in the group. The most impressive national performances came from Sweden (7.26 per cent of sales), Germany (6.80 per cent), Switzerland (6.78 per cent) and Japan (5.90 per cent). The gap between the UK and other countries becomes wider still when R&D is related to profits and dividends. R&D spending by the international top 200 averaged 101 per cent of pre-tax profits and 283 per cent of dividends; equivalent figures for the UK companies were 29 per cent of profits and 72 per cent of dividends. (*Financial Times*, 17 June 1994)

As to the level of workforce training, the relatively poor position of Britain in comparative terms has been increasingly recognized in recent years. Table 5.2 provides some relevant information. Although international comparisons remain unfavourable to Britain, it should be noted that the percentage of employees receiving job-related training in Britain rose from 9 to 14 per cent in the years 1984–9;[8] more recent figures indicate that some 13.6 per cent of the workforce received training in 1993.[9]

Table 5.2    *Vocational qualifications of the workforce in Britain and selected other countries (per cent of all economically active persons)*

|  | Britain 1989 | France 1988 | Germany 1988 | Netherlands 1989 | Switzerland 1991 |
|---|---|---|---|---|---|
| University degrees | 11 | 7 | 11 | 8 | 11 |
| Intermediate vocational qualifications | 25 | 40 | 63 | 57 | 66 |
| of which | | | | | |
|    Technician | 7 | 7 | 7 | 19 | 9 |
|    Craft | 18 | 33 | 56 | 38 | 57 |
| No vocational qualifications | 64 | 53 | 26 | 35 | 23 |

*Source*: S.J. Prais, 'Economic performance and education: the nature of Britain's deficiencies', National Institute of Economic and Social Research Discussion Paper, 52, 1993, p. 9.

This low-labour-cost competitive strategy is closely bound up with a number of related characteristics, namely (i) a major priority being given to shareholder interests; (ii) a strong responsiveness to (internal and external) short-run financial performance measures; and, as noted earlier, (iii) a limited role being accorded to employee-management issues and considerations in strategic-level decision-making. The widespread strength of these 'facts of organizational life' in Britain are well illustrated by the wording of the following item of news: 'Fisons, the troubled pharmaceuticals and scientific equipment group, is *planning plant closures and large scale redundancies in a bid to restore confidence in the company*' (*Financial Times*, 20 December 1993, my emphasis). Similarly, it was recently reported that financial analysts are particularly pleased and impressed with Pilkington's management in cutting costs by some £42m. in the six months to September 1994; about 600 jobs went in the first half of the year, with a further 1,000 scheduled to go before the end of the year (*Financial Times*, 23 November 1994). As Pfeffer has noted (admittedly in the US context) this sort of language certainly tells us something about the relatively low priority attached to managing the workforce as a source of competitive advantage.[10] Indeed, it has been aptly noted that British and US managers 'can downsize, declutter, de-layer and divest better than any others' (*Financial Times*, 23 November 1994). The role of the low-labour-cost competitive strategy (and its related dimensions) as a constraint on the adoption and maintenance of employment-management innova-tions will be a major theme developed in the remainder of this chapter.

Turning now to the second element of the Goverment's labour market strategy, it must be initially recognized that an evaluation of it is a far from straightforward matter, simply because one does not know what would have occurred in its absence. This being said, the work of a number of economists has shown that many labour market *outcomes* have not been in line with the stated aims or objectives of government policy during the 1980s. One rela-tively early study suggested a mixed record of performance (for the years 1979–89), with the successes being the reduced level of inflation and the improvement in productivity, but with the costs being increased unemployment and increased income inequality.[11] Table 5.3 lists some of the leading labour market indicators drawn from this particular study.

More recently, a comprehensive study of labour market out-comes in Britain in the 1980s reached the following conclusion:

> The Thatcherite reforms succeeded in their goals of weakening union power; may have marginally increased employment and wage responsiveness to market conditions and may have increased self-employment. They were accompanied by a substantial im-provement in the labour market position of women. But the reforms failed to improve the responsiveness of real wages to unemploy-ment; they were associated with a slower transition from non-employment to employment for men; a devastating loss in full time jobs for male workers; produced substantial seemingly non-competitive increases in wage inequality. While we cannot rule out the possibility that the reforms created the preconditions for an economic 'miracle' in the mid-1990s there is little in the data to support such a sanguine reading of the British experience. Higher inequality and poverty and lower full time employment are not normally viewed as an ideal stepping stage for economic success.[12]

In summary, it would seem difficult to conclude from the evidence of this section that the associated costs of the institu-tional vacuum have in any substantial measure been offset by a more efficient set of labour market outcomes that has, in turn, enhanced the larger competitive performance of the British economy. Indeed it would appear that we have something like the following situation:

1   Government policy has helped undermine the traditional institutional props of union membership and collective bargaining coverage, but has done relatively little to encourage their replacement: tax incentives for the adoption of employee share-ownership schemes constitute something of an exception in this regard, which will be discussed later in this chapter.

2   The Government's support for the traditional low-labour-cost competitive strategy has reinforced the limited organizational importance attached to employment-management issues. And

Table 5.3   *Selected UK economic statistics*

|  | 1977 | 1981 | 1988 |
|---|---|---|---|
| GDP[a] | 100.0 | 96.7 | 121.0 |
| Manufacturing output | 100.0 | 85.9 | 107.8 |
| Output/head | 100.0 | 99.9 | 121.3 |
| Manufacturing output/head | 100.0 | 99.5 | 148.1 |
| Unemployment rate | 4.9 | 9.4 | 8.6 |
| Long-term employment rate (more than 12 months) | 1.2 | 2.1 | 3.5 |
| Retail price inflation | 13.4 | 11.9 | 4.9 |
| Real earnings | 100.0 | 105.3 | 126.0 |
| Real earnings (male manuals, lowest decile) | 100.0 | 102.1 | 107.0 |
| Profit share (% of GDP)[b] | 20.4 | 16.5 | 21.0 |
| Public sector debt repayment (% of GDP)[c] | −6.4 | −4.1 | 2.4 |
| Government expenditure (% of GDP)[c] | 43.4 | 46.1 | 38.6 |
| Tax revenue (% of GDP)[c] | 34.1 | 37.8 | 37.2 |
| Current account (% of GDP)[c] | −0.3 | 2.7 | −3.1 |

[a] Average of income, output and expenditure measures.
[b] At factor cost.
[c] At market prices.

*Source*: C. Bean and J. Symons, 'Ten years of Mrs T.', Centre for Labour Economics, LSE, Discussion Paper 370, January 1990, p. 60.

this, in turn, has limited the incentive of management to 'replace' the declining role of collective bargaining with HRM practices.

3   The resulting institutional vacuum has entailed employee equity costs both in terms of enhanced wage inequality and the limited development of formal procedural arrangements (covering employee consultation, involvement and information-sharing matters) in the non-union sector.

4   The institutional vacuum may also be a source of costs or missed benefits to management in organizations. For instance, one recent study reported that employee-participation arrangements can strongly and positively shape attitudes of employees towards their organization, and yet 'the most striking feature of our data is just how rare it is for employees to be involved in this type of decision'.[13]

5   The low-wage competitive strategy and the labour market deregulation reforms have yielded few obvious competitive advantages to Britain to date, and are arguably even less likely to do so in the future.

If one is to improve efficiency and equity in the British labour market there is clearly a strong case for seeking to fill the institutional gap that has opened up as a result of the declining role of collective bargaining. But for public policy to assist in this regard it will have to, first, identify the constraints on the diffusion of employee relations innovations and, secondly, develop instruments with the potential to offset these constraints. As a step towards the first task the next section reviews some of the leading lessons to emerge from periodic attempts to supplement the role of collective bargaining over the course of time.

## SOME PERIODIC ATTEMPTS TO SUPPLEMENT COLLECTIVE BARGAINING

Until the 1980s there had never been any real question raised in management or policy-making circles about seeking an institutional alternative to collective bargaining. At most, as we saw in Chapter 1, there were attempts to 'reform' collective bargaining (that is, to decentralize it, and enhance the regulation of its processes and outcomes) and/or supplement it with mechanisms designed to address the integrative, as opposed to distributive, side of the employment relationship. These periodic, supplementary mechanisms have included (essentially in the order in which they occurred) profit-sharing schemes, joint consultative committees, organization development and change initiatives, and trade union directors on company boards – though admittedly this last was more a theme for discussion than a matter of actual organizational practice, when compared with the other three sets of innovations.

A review of the historical record of these initiatives reveals three basic findings: (1) a substantial number of firms that introduced them did not sustain them over the course of time; (2) the extent of the spread or diffusion of such innovations across a broad cross-section of industry was relatively limited; and (3) within large, multi-establishment organizations such innovations did not spread uniformly or evenly throughout the organization as a whole. These findings, which are highlighted in this section, point to the existence and strength of various constraints on the processes of institutionalizing and diffusing industrial relations innovations in Britain. And it is these constraints that practitioners and policy-makers will increasingly have to address if the existing institutional vacuum in the present national system is to be filled.

Historically, the first of our employee relations innovations was profit-sharing arrangements, with the adoption of such schemes being particularly associated with the 1860s and 1870s, the late 1880s and early 1890s, and the years immediately prior to the First World War;[14] some 88 schemes were, for instance, initiated in the years 1889–92. Early employer interest in profit-sharing was undoubtedly stimulated in many cases by a desire to limit the growth of union organization, although the latter-stage schemes seemed more concerned to try to enhance the integrative side of the employment relationship by reducing 'them vs us' attitudes and behaviour. However, the relatively limited institutionalization and diffusion of these arrangements over the course of time were well evidenced by an enquiry in the late 1920s, which revealed that:[15]

- The number of profit-sharing schemes initiated in all industries covered only a small proportion of all the firms in those industries.
- Nearly 50 per cent of all schemes known to have been started had been discontinued.

- Only the gas industry was an exception in the above regards.

The second mechanism designed to supplement collective bargaining was joint consultative committees, which again sought to address subject areas where there was allegedly the potential for co-operation in the employment relationship. As with profit-sharing arrangements, the establishment of such committees (sometimes called joint production committees, particularly in the war years) was disproportionately concentrated in particular periods of time, notably 1916–22 and the years of the Second World War and immediately following it; in 1943, for instance, it was estimated that there were some 4,000 joint production committees (covering some 2.5 million employees) in the engineering and allied industries.[16] However, in the 1950s and, more particularly, the 1960s, such committees were overtaken by the emergence and development of shop-floor-level bargaining arrangements based on shop stewards, which variously resulted in the committees being formally discontinued, being relegated to an increasingly minor role (in terms of the importance of the subject-matter discussed), or becoming *de facto* bargaining bodies. For instance, a study of the engineering industry suggested that (1) only about 20 per cent of (federated) engineering establishments had a joint production committee in the early 1960s and (2) the number of establishments with such a committee had declined by a third from the mid-1950s.[17]

The 1970s saw the emergence of some more specialist (in subject-matter) consultative committees, most notably in the area of health and safety following the passage of enabling legislation in 1974. There was also some debate, not to say controversy, as to whether joint consultative committees were experiencing some sort of revival in the 1970s.[18] However, since then it has become apparent that the number of joint consultative committees essentially plateaued in the early 1980s, and has since then declined (see Table 3.3).

A more diffuse set of employee relations initiatives occurred in a relatively small sub-set of well known, 'progressive' organizations in the 1960s and 1970s. These initiatives frequently spread out from early productivity bargaining exercises, sought to enhance both productivity and job satisfaction, were sometimes influenced by socio-technical systems theory (with its emphasis on semi-autonomous work groups), and often involved experiments in job enlargement/enrichment/rotation that were variously labelled organization-development/change or quality-of-working-life programmes. Although never representing a broad-based movement across British industry as a whole (which in itself is an instructive finding), such programmes in certain well-known companies such as Shell and ICI nevertheless yielded some interesting insights and lessons, such as the following:

- The spread or diffusion of such programmes in large-sized, multi-establishment organizations was frequently relatively limited, as a result of factors such as middle management indifference or opposition. For instance, in ICI the initial centrepiece of the organization-development programme was the MUPS productivity bargain. But Pettigrew has shown that only 5 per cent of the ICI workforce was covered by MUPS three years after the central enabling agreement was signed with the union.[19]

- Top-down, senior-management-led, organization-wide change programmes frequently generated considerable intra-management opposition (as in the ICI case), which hindered the process of implementing and sustaining change. As a consequence many organization change and development programmes now emphasize much more of a decentralized, incremental approach to their introduction and operation.[20]

- Any short-run benefits from such innovations may not be fully or even adequately sustained over time. This was very much the lesson of experience in Shell.[21]

- Union attitudes towards schemes designed to enhance job satisfaction were somewhat ambivalent in nature, with concerns being expressed by the unions about the processes of introducing such schemes, their potential for 'dividing' the workforce and the nature of their relationship with existing collective bargaining arrangements.[22]

Finally, some reference should be made to the 1970s discussion and debate concerning the potential role and value of having some degree of trade union representation on company boards of directors. In contrast to the three measures previously discussed, the interest here was not so much to complement collective bargaining by addressing the integrative side of the employment relationship, but rather to complement it by extending its reach into the strategic level of decision-making within organizations. In their evidence to the Bullock Committee of Inquiry all unions emphasized the prime importance they attached to collective bargaining, although there was some disagreement among them as to whether union directors would complement or compromise the role of collective bargaining. Box 5.1 illustrates two differing views on this matter.

The evidence to the Bullock Committee of Inquiry, together with the experiments in British Steel and the Post Office,[23] highlighted the following set of findings and issues:

---

**Box 5.1**   *Two union views on trade union directors*

1   (GMWU) There has to be a significant development of trade union machinery in the private sector towards the creation of company level machinery . . . at the point where strategic decisions are really made . . . it is at the company level that the major decisions are made. The creation of collective bargaining machinery at company level is a necessary prerequisite to any further institutional development on industrial democracy.

2   (EETPU) First, there is the institutional impossibility of separating the boardroom consultation from the potential negotiating implications behind the issues under discussion. Second, there is the irreconcilable split loyalties of the worker directors themselves. They will find it immensely difficult to separate their boardroom responsibilities dictated by business priorities from their representative functions derived from their relationship with the workforce . . . Far better in the interests of those affected by a managerial decision that the responsibility for the decision is firmly laid at the management's door; then the collective bargaining machinery can oppose and moderate the impact of the decision when necessary.

*Source: Report of the Committee of Inquiry on Industrial Democracy,* Cmnd 6706, London, HMSO, 1977, pp. 36 and 39–40.

---

1   A very considerable strength of management opposition to union involvement in strategic level decision-making processes, justified largely on the grounds of management responsibility to shareholder interests and the lack of technical expertise of union representatives.

2   The doubtfulness of the assumption that the board level is the key senior management strategic-level decision-making body, at least in many organizations.

3   The limited extent to which industrial relations and human resource management decisions are viewed by senior managers as strategic decisions.

4   The tendency in practice of union directors to confine their discussions and contribution overwhelmingly to industrial relations and employment-related matters.

5   The potential for other directors, if necessary, to displace discussions and decisions concerning key strategic matters to more informal decision-making circles outside the boardroom.

In view of the above it was not surprising to find that none of the experiments with union directors in Britain resulted in a significant 'add on' to collective bargaining, in the sense of providing an influential union input into strategic management decision-making processes. This sort of finding has been echoed in research conducted in other countries such as Australia and the USA,[24] with only the (West) German experience producing a much stronger, more positive assessment of the role and contribution of worker (union) directors. This divergence of findings between Germany and the rest may reflect:

● the use of rather different criteria for assessing the contribution of worker (union) directors in different systems;

● the fact that worker directors are much more of a system-wide norm in Germany, whereas in other countries they have constituted only isolated, atypical experiments (that is, the greater system-wide acceptance of the role in Germany might help account for their more positive impact); and

● the greater institutional support for the role in German organizations, owing to the existence of complementary bodies, such as the works council and the labour director.

In view of this last observation, it is interesting to note that the current interest in the employee relations practices of German organizations centres much more around works councils than worker directors. This theme is pursued in Chapter 7.

The existence of constraints on the processes of diffusing and institutionalizing employee relations innovations is not a matter of historical curiosity. Rather it constitutes a matter of major contemporary importance. For example, a number of commentators have highlighted the existence of such constraints in limiting the general take-up of HRM practices in Britain,[25] an observation clearly borne out by some of the findings reported in Chapters 3 and 4. Indeed, a recent survey of some 62 organizations indicated that some one in ten planned to discontinue a current employee involvement initiative in the near future.[26] Box 5.2 illustrates the limited spread of a recent employee involvement initiative within one large organization.

## THE CONSTRAINTS ON DIFFUSION

The volume of systematic empirical research concerning the constraints on the diffusion and institutionalization of employee relations innovations within national systems of industrial relations is very limited. In fact the most impressive empirical research concerning diffusion in the employment-management area has been across national systems. This comparative (inter-systems) research has revealed that national industrial relations systems characterized by (1) relatively centralized bargaining arrangements, (2) relatively cohesive union and employer confederations and (3) relatively co-operative union–management relationships have the greatest diffusion capability.[27] The sort of findings in Table 5.4 appear broadly consistent with this set of observations.

Increasingly, however, researchers are beginning to identify some of the constraints that have limited the spread of employee relations innovations within individual organizations and between organizations in individual systems.[28] Industrial relations researchers have contributed to this work by highlighting the relevance of the following sorts of factors:

• union opposition or ambivalence;

## Box 5.2    *The limited spread of continuous improvement within an organization*

This organization is a unionized one, with some 1,800 employees. It has long had close dealings (as both a customer and supplier) with a particular American company which has introduced a continuous improvement programme, with a strong emphasis on 'employee empowerment'. The American company has persuaded the British one to consider the case for adopting a similar programme of organizational change. To this end senior management discussions (involving a consultant paid by the American company) have taken place between the two organizations, representatives of the British company have visited plants in the US to observe the practices involved and a training manual has been provided by the American company. In mid-1993 the British organization launched a training programme in continuous improvement principles, with a strong emphasis on team or group problem-solving. The intention is to train some 150 facilitators in these principles. In some nine months they have trained 60 facilitators, although these are disproportionately concentrated in one division or business area of the organizations. This particular division is the most profitable part of the organization, and is headed by a director with a strong prior commitment to the notion of employee empowerment who has been assigned a target of raising turnover by a factor of three in the next four years. In this particular division, problems have arisen with suggestions for improvement from problem-solving groups outpacing the capacity to implement the recommendations, and with some of the older middle managers feeling threatened by the nature of the recommendations being advanced. Indeed a number of these managers have requested that the organization should formally define the term 'employee empowerment' in terms of the specific duties and responsibilities of employees and managers. In contrast, the continuous improvement programme has hardly touched the other three business areas of the organization, with few facilitators having been trained; and the few that have been trained have not yet established problem-solving groups.

Table 5.4  *The extent of employee involvement in the introduction of new technology*

|  | Planning stage | Implementation stage |
|---|---|---|
| *Top rank* | Denmark, Germany | Denmark, Germany |
| *Middle rank* | Ireland, Netherlands, Belgium | Ireland, Netherlands, UK, Greece, France, Spain |
| *Lowest rank* | UK, France, Spain, Greece, Italy, Luxemburg, Portugal | Portugal, Italy, Luxemburg |

*Source*: European Foundation for Improvement in Living and Working Conditions, *Workplace Involvement in Technological Innovation in the European Community*, 1993.

- the relative absence of other supportive, mutually reinforcing policies and practices;
- the offsetting power of collective bargaining;
- limited knowledge of the innovations; and
- the turnover of key people.[29]

The contents of Box 5.3 provide an illustration of how the promotion and turnover of a key manager can undermine the longer-term staying power of employee relations innovations.

The sort of factors specific to employee relations listed above are certainly relevant constraints on the processes of diffusing and maintaining innovations. This is indicated by Table 5.5. However, they are arguably not nearly as powerful as the ones which derive from the larger environment and structure of the organization. In essence it is a bundle of interrelated factors centring around the low-labour-cost competitive strategy that constitute the major constraints on the diffusion and maintenance of innovations in the employee-management area; these factors include (1) the strong commitment to serving shareholder interests, (2) the strength of short-run financial performance considerations and measures, and (3) the limited priority attached to employee-management considerations in strategic decision-making processes. The role of these factors in explaining the historically limited extent of workforce training in Britain has been strongly emphasized,[30] although arguably their role runs much more broadly and deeply throughout the employee-relations domain. Indeed the role and strength of these larger organizational factors has been demonstrated in systems similar to Britain's.[31] For example, a recent study in Canada reported that around 30 per cent of employee-participation and incentive-based pay systems that existed in 1985 had been discontinued by 1991.[32]

The low-labour-cost competitive strategy of British firms (mentioned earlier in the chapter) is associated with relatively high profit margins, high returns to investors and the lowest share of value added going to employees.[33] For instance, a study in the early 1990s revealed that average profit margins (across eight industrial sectors) were 9.8 per cent in the UK, 4.2 per cent in Germany, 7.1 per cent in France and 5.4 per cent in Italy.[34] The distribution of value added revealed by this study is set out in Table 5.6.

This strong responsiveness to shareholder interests translates into the importance of meeting short-run financial performance

---

### Box 5.3   *Career development practices and employment innovations: a conversation**

*Bob:*   You know I will be leaving this plant after two years. My promotion has been strongly influenced by the reputation attached to the employee involvement scheme that I have initiated here. As my successor, I hope you will keep it going, and indeed push hard for its further development, as its potential is very considerable.

John:   Why should I bother keeping it going? It is very much regarded, quite rightly, throughout the company as your pet project. What's in it for me if I push to keep it going? I want promotion too, and this company only rewards initiators, not finishers who fine-tune the details of other people's work. I need to start something myself – have it seen as my project – and that's how I will get the visibility to get on.

* This particular conversation never actually took place. Rather it captures the essence of a number of private conversations I have been party to in various organizations.

Table 5.5   *The limited maintenance of quality circles in Great Britain*

1   32 out of 127 organizations had suspended their complete quality circle programmes. These suspensions occurred within three years of introduction. Redundancies and restructuring were among the major reasons for this decision.

2   78 out of the 127 organizations had suspended some individual quality circles. (This involved some 25 per cent of all the circles originally established.)   Most of these suspensions occurred within 18 months of establishing the circles. Redundancies/restructuring, labour turnover and middle management/supervisor lack of co-operation were among the major factors involved.

*Source*: R. Collard and B. Dale, 'Quality circles' in K. Sisson (ed.), *Personnel Management in Britain*, Oxford, Blackwell, 1989, pp. 367–8.

objectives and measures. A number of recent studies of corporate governance, for example, have argued that British firms are more subject to short-run pressures from the stock market, are more vulnerable to the threat of (hostile) takeover and have less longer-term constructive relationships with banks than their counterparts in Germany or Japan.[35] These external financial pressures are strongly mirrored in the internal management structure of British

Table 5.6   *Distribution of value added across countries*

| Country | Companies listed | Investor share (%) | Employee share (%) |
|---|---|---|---|
| UK | 201 | 8.1 | 60.2 |
| Spain | 10 | 8.1 | 65.6 |
| Italy | 25 | 7.3 | 64.1 |
| Belgium | 17 | 6.8 | 63.3 |
| Netherlands | 35 | 5.0 | 66.9 |
| Denmark | 15 | 4.3 | 69.8 |
| France | 111 | 3.7 | 67.2 |
| Germany | 81 | 2.7 | 75.7 |
| Ireland | 4 | 2.6 | 67.5 |

*Source*: Cited in C. Hendry, *Human Resource Strategies for International Growth*, London, Routledge, 1994, p. 145.

Table 5.7    *The salaries of finance and personnel directors, London banks/finance houses, 1994*

|  | Average salary | Median salary | Upper quartile | Lower quartile |
| --- | --- | --- | --- | --- |
| Finance director | 81,972 | 75,765 | 86,000 | 62,001 |
| Personnel director | 69,927 | 70,000 | 80,000 | 55,000 |

*Source*: *Financial Times*, 23 February 1994, p. 14.

firms. For instance, it is well known that accountants are strongly represented on company boards in Britain.[36] Moreover, if salary constitutes a reasonable proxy for the importance of a functional area then it is no surprise to find that financial directors earn considerably more than their personnel counterparts. Some recent figures to this effect are set out in Table 5.7.

The differing competitive strategies (with their associated characteristics) of organizations in Britain and the US on the one hand and Japan and Germany on the other have been increasingly highlighted.[37] In general the view is the latter countries have placed much more emphasis on human resource practices as a route to competitive success. That is, they emphasize product innovation or quality enhancement strategies, rather than the low-labour-cost approach of Britain and the US, which necessitates more priority being given to industrial relations and HRM matters.[38] Is there a useful single measure of this differing priority? In seeking to account for variation in workforce training across national systems, Kochan and Osterman have argued as follows:

> One would expect that firms which provide more stable employment will engage in more training. In part this flows from the standard human capital argument concerning the need to retain workers in order to capture the returns to training. However, the reality is more subtle since the argument also runs in reverse: longer tenures and more training are parts of, and are caused by, the larger set of human resource policies ...[39]

In short, if one can generalize from this training-based argument one should find employment tenures on average being longer in

Table 5.8   *Enterprise tenure, selected countries, 1991*

|  | Germany | Japan | UK | USA |
|---|---|---|---|---|
| Average tenure (years), all persons | 10.4 | 10.9 | 7.9 | 6.7 |
| Median tenure (years), all persons | 7.5 | 8.2 | 4.4 | 3.0 |

*Source: OECD Employment Outlook*, Paris, OECD, July 1993, p. 121.

Germany and Japan than in Britain and the US. Some relevant supportive figures are contained in Table 5.8.

To summarize, the constraints on the institutionalization and diffusion of employee relations innovations can apparently be broadly categorized into two groups: (1) those that are relatively specific to the industrial relations domain (for example union opposition, turnover of key individuals) and (2) those that derive from the nature of the larger business environment and organization. The major potential problem for producing change in the present system is that, while the former are likely to be the easier to change (although even here the difficulties should not be underestimated), it is the latter group that it is more important to change. The issue of future change is pursued in later chapters (particularly Chapters 6 and 8), whereas here we examine the range of existing policy instruments that have been used to try to assist the processes of diffusion.

## SOME PUBLIC POLICY INSTRUMENTS TO ASSIST DIFFUSION

One relatively long-standing instrument of public policy designed to assist the processes of diffusing industrial relations innovations in Britain has been the issuing of codes of practice. In essence such documents, issued by government departments and agencies, define 'good practice' in a particular subject area and offer a set of guidelines for the effective design, implementation and operation of the recommended practice. These codes of practice are not legally binding (although in some subject areas, such as dismissals, they may be a relevant input to the deliberations of industrial tribunals), and essentially embody the assumption or view that diffusion is constrained by a lack of knowledge on the part of potential adopters.

There has been very little research on the extent to which organizations obtain copies of such codes of practice and implement their recommended approach. However, one sample study found that (i) only a small minority (15 per cent) had obtained a copy of a particular code of practice issued in the preceding six months or so, and (ii) those who had obtained a copy were a relatively innovatory sub-set of the sample, who had already introduced (at least in some form) the recommended policy arrangement;[40] though undoubtedly codes of practice that may be introduced into industrial tribunal hearings have been more widely obtained and implemented.

A second instrument of public policy, which was initially used by the Work Research Unit of the Department of Employment and subsequently ACAS in the 1980s and 1990s, has been the establishment, at least in certain areas of the country, of inter-firm networks designed to share experiences and generate lessons for others. Such networks currently in existence are concerned with QWL innovations (broadly defined) and TQM approaches. The potential value of such inter-firm networks is suggested by the argument that there are severe limitations to an organizational change model that involves simply the interaction between human resource managers and line managers in single organizations. Instead, what is required is a coalitional (multiple stakeholder) model of organizational change in which a structure and process for promoting the learning and transfer of innovations across individual organizational boundaries is particularly prominent.[41] Moreover, networks of the type discussed here are potentially important in this regard, as they involve sources or flows of information that embody two kinds of credibility that are particularly appealing to organizational practitioners:[42] (1) 'safety credibility' (this person/organization is my peer, is like me and has no axe to grind in giving me the information) and (2) 'professional' or 'technical' credibility (this person/organization know(s) what they are talking about).

There are, however, two more pessimistic views about such networks, which are essentially as follows:

- Such networks have a high probability of being unlikely to survive the test of time, particularly in the face of the turnover of leading individuals associated with establishing them in the first place.

- Such networks are over-homogeneous bodies, involving essentially similar, like-minded (that is, 'good practice') organizations basically talking among themselves, with relatively little incentive or ability to reach out, draw in and influence other, very different types of organizations. That is, they essentially involve the converted speaking to the converted.

The latter view was to a considerable extent confirmed in a recent study of two such inter-firm networks, which found that (1) their membership was relatively homogeneous in nature and (2) the members of the networks already had (before joining) a relatively comprehensive HRM policy mix in place.[43] Some of the key findings in these regards are set out in Table 5.9.

In summary, research on both of these instruments for diffusing industrial relations and HRM innovations is very limited, but what is available suggests that they are only reaching the converted. That is, they are not reaching or drawing in establishments from a broad cross-section of industry, but rather are limited in coverage or membership terms to a small, atypical sub-

Table 5.9 *Two QWL inter-firm networks*

---

- 86% of management members were from the HRM functional area.
- 84% were in the manufacturing sector, 78% were part of multi-establishment organizations, the mean establishment size was some 635, and 92% recognized trade unions for collective bargaining purposes (mean union density level was 70%).
- 46% had joint consultative committees, 92% had joint health and safety committees, 51% had team working arrangements, 38% had single-status (all-salaried workforce) terms and conditions, 24% had quality circles, and 32% had conducted employee attitude surveys.
- Just under half (49%) reported that they had introduced a new QWL-type innovation since joining the network (about half of these attributed this change, at least in part, to network membership), while 54% reported that they had reformed or modified an existing QWL-type innovation since joining the network (again about half attributed this change, at least in part, to network membership).

---

*Source*: P.B. Beaumont and P.J.R. Richards, 'Inter-firm networks: seeking to sustain and diffuse QWL innovations', Report for ACAS Wales, 1993.

set of organizations with an above-average incentive/ability to innovate on their own initiative.

Is there another public policy instrument that has been used and has the potential to break out of this sort of closed circle type of situation? In recent years tax incentives have been used to encourage the take-up and spread of profit-sharing, employee share-ownership schemes, and profit-related pay arrangements; such incentives have regularly featured in a series of Finance Acts in Britain from the late 1970s. An illustrative example is provided in Table 5.10.

To some commentators this is one of the relatively few positive industrial relations policy measures taken by the Government in recent years;[44] – positive in the sense of seeking to encourage alternative arrangements in the face of the declining role of collective bargaining. Moreover, the available evidence clearly indicates the quite noticeable growth of such schemes in Britain throughout the 1980s,[45] with further evidence suggesting that such growth has been stimulated by the availability of tax incentives.[46]

The pattern of diffusion of such schemes in the years 1984–90 has been examined,[47] with particular attention being given to the

Table 5.10 *Tax incentives for employee share ownership*

---

*1980 Finance Act – Save As You Earn (SAYE) schemes*

- All full-time employees with five or more years of service must be eligible to participate on similar terms. Other employees may be included in the scheme if the company wishes, but all employees who take part must do so on similar terms.

- Participants must take out a SAYE contract in order to fund the purchase of the shares. The contract must be for an agreed amount per month of between £20 and £250 for a period of five years.

- The share options may be exercised using the savings made under the linked savings contract. No income tax is payable on options exercised at the end of the five-year savings period.

- Total number of schemes approved March 1992 – 1,058; number of employees to whom shares were allocated in 1991–92 – 470,000; average per employee – £2,900.

---

*Source*: G. Smith, 'Employee share schemes in Britain', *Employment Gazette*, April, 1993, p. 154.

roles of the existing employee–management relationship and the larger industry influence as factors in shaping the take-up of these schemes. The results obtained provided strong support for the influence of these factors. Table 5.11 presents the basic findings concerning the role of the employee–management relationship. It indicates that the earlier adopters of employee share-ownership schemes were characterized by 'good' (as perceived by management) employee–management relations, with subsequent diffusion occurring to establishments with poorer perceived relationships.

The results of this particular study, when combined with information on the spread of employee share-ownership schemes in Britain[48] and Canada,[49] suggested the following implications:

1   Employee share-ownership schemes spread more widely in Britain (where tax incentives were available) than in Canada (where no such incentives existed) in the 1980s.

2   The tax incentives in Britain have not produced an essentially random diffusion of such arrangements across establishments (that is, their spread was uneven).

3   The fact that such arrangements were increasingly adopted by establishments with poorer quality employee–management

Table 5.11   *The diffusion pattern of employee share-ownership schemes (private sector)*

|  | % of employees belonging to share-ownership schemes and % of plants | | | |
| | 1984 | | 1990 | |
| Management–employee relations at workplace | Employees | Plants | Employees | Plants |
| --- | --- | --- | --- | --- |
| 1   (very good) | 4.46 | 41.9 | 5.54 | 32.8 |
| 2   (quite good) | 5.31 | 43.6 | 13.76 | 22.9 |
| 3   (good) | 1.77 | 10.3 | 10.81 | 37.2 |
| 4   (quite poor) | 2.12 | 2.7 | 12.92 | 6.1 |
| 5–7 (poor to very poor) | 0.08 | 1.5 | 7.14 | 1.0 |

*Source*: P.B. Beaumont and R.I.D. Harris, 'The pattern of diffusion of employee share ownership schemes in Britain: some key findings', *International Journal of Human Resource Management*, 6 (May), 1995.

'policy success'. This is because the tax incentives may have helped spread this innovation beyond the relatively small sub-set of 'best practice' organizations with an above-average incentive/ability to innovate on their own initiative.

4    The role of the 'industry demonstration' effect was powerful, with the probability of an individual establishment adopting such arrangements being strongly influenced by the proportion of establishments in the industry that had adopted the innovation. This could be an important influence in the maintenance (or not) of such arrangements over the course of time.

## SUMMARY

This chapter has argued that the institutional vacuum in the British industrial relations system needs to be filled for a variety of reasons, and has examined earlier attempts to supplement collective bargaining with a view to identifying some of the issues that practitioners and policy-makers will need to address in this attempt. Furthermore, some consideration has been given to the performance of existing public policy instruments that can be drawn upon in this task. Among the leading individual findings and arguments presented were the following:

- The major constraints on the maintenance and diffusion of employee relations innovations derive from the larger strategies and structures of the organization.

- Codes of practice and inter-firm networks must seek to reach and draw in a much broader range of establishments, in particular reaching into the non-union employment sector, where voluntarily initiated HRM practices are relatively limited.

- Tax incentives for employee relations innovations would appear to have considerable potential for helping to fill the institutional vacuum. This is because they appear to have helped spread employee share-ownership schemes to an increasingly heterogeneous (at least in terms of perceived employee–management relations) group of establishments over time.

# REFERENCES

1 W. Brown, 'The consequences of dismantling British collective bargaining', Labour Relations Agency, Belfast, *Review of Employment Topics*, 2, June 1994, pp. 1–11.

2 A. Gosling and S. Machin, 'Trade unions and the dispersion of earnings in UK establishments, 1980–1990', Centre for Economic Performance, LSE, Discussion Paper 140, May 1993.

3 P. Blyton and P. Turnbull, *The Dynamics of Employee Relations*, London, Macmillan, 1994.

4 P.B. Beaumont (1990) *Change in Industrial Relations*, London, Routledge, 1990, Chapter 4.

5 M. Porter, *The Competitive Advantage of Nations*, London, Macmillan, 1990, pp. 494–6.

6 M. Smith, 'UK manufacturing output and trade performance', *Midland Bank Review*, Autumn 1986, pp. 8–16.

7 L. Thurow, *Head to Head*, New York, Morrow, 1992.

8 *Social Trends 21*, London, HMSO, 1991, p. 80.

9 Department of Employment, *Labour Market Quarterly Report*, May 1994, p. 7.

10 J. Pfeffer, *Competitive Advantage through People*, Boston, Harvard Business School Press, 1994, Chapter 4.

11 C. Bean and J. Symons, 'Ten years of Mrs T', Centre for Labour Economics, LSE, Discussion Paper 370, January 1990.

12 D. Blanchflower and R. Freeman, 'Did the Thatcher reforms change British labour market performance?', Centre for Economic Performance, LSE, Discussion Paper 168, August 1993, p. 2.

13 D. Gaillie and M. White, *Employee Commitment and the Skills Revolution*, London, PSI, 1993.

14 P. Brannan, *Authority and Participation in Industry*, London, Batsford, 1983, pp. 35–7.

15 Ministry of Labour, 'Profit sharing and labour co-partnership in 1928', *Ministry of Labour Gazette*, 37 (7), 1929, p. 234.

16 Brannan, *Authority and Participation*, p. 44.

17 A. Marsh, *Industrial Relations in Engineering*, Oxford, Pergamon, 1965, p. 110.

18 P.B. Beaumont, *Change in Industrial Relations*, London, Routledge, 1990, pp. 231–2.

19 A. Pettigrew, *The Awakening Giant*, Oxford, Blackwell, 1985, p. 88.

20 See, for example, L. Hunter and P.B. Beaumont, 'Implementing TQM: top down or bottom up?', *Industrial Relations Journal*, 24 (4), 1993, pp. 319–20.

21  F. Blackler and C. Brown, *Whatever Happened to Shell's New Philosophy of Management?*, London, Saxon House, 1980.

22  K. Graham, 'Union attitudes to job satisfaction', in M. Weir (ed.), *Job Satisfaction*, London, Fontana, 1976, pp. 265–72.

23  Brannan, *Authority and Participation*, Chapter 6.

24  T.H. Hammer, S.C. Currall and R.N. Stern, 'Worker representation on boards of directors: a study of competing roles', *Industrial and Labor Relations Review*, 44 (4), 1991, pp. 661–80.

25  J. Storey and K. Sisson, 'Limits to transformation: human resource management in the British context', *Industrial Relations Journal*, 20, 1989.

26  *Industrial Relations Review and Report*, 545, October 1993.

27  See, for example, R.E. Walton, *Innovating to Compete*, San Francisco, Jossey Bass, 1987.

28  See, for example, David Levine, 'Public policy implications of imperfections in the market for worker participation', *Economic and Industrial Democracy*, 13, 1992, pp. 183–206; R.E. Cole, B. Bacdayan and B.J. White, 'Quality, participation and competitiveness', *California Management Review*, 1993, pp. 68–81.

29  G. Strauss, 'Workers' participation in management', in J.F. Hartley and G.M. Stephenson (eds), *Employee Relations: The Psychology of Influences and Control at Work*, Oxford, Blackwell, 1992, pp. 291–313.

30  E. Keep, 'Corporate training strategies: the vital component?', in J. Storey (ed.), *New Perspectives on Human Resource Management*, London, Routledge, 1989, pp. 109–25.

31  T.A. Kochan and P. Osterman, *The Mutual Gains Enterprise*, Cambridge, Mass., Harvard Business School Press, 1994.

32  G. Betcherman, N. Leckie and A. Verma, 'HRM innovations in Canada: evidence from establishment surveys', paper presented at the Canadian Industrial Relations Association Meeting, Ottawa, 1993.

33  C. Hendry, *Human Resource Strategies for International Growth*, London, Routledge, 1994, pp. 144–6.

34  Ibid., p. 145.

35  J. Charkham, *Keeping Good Company: A Study of Corporate Governance in Five Countries*, Oxford, Oxford University Press, 1993.

36  P. Armstrong, 'Limits and possibilities for HRM in an age of management accountancy', in Storey (ed.), *New Perspectives on HRM*, p. 157.

37  See, for example, L. Thorow, *Head to Head*, New York, Morrow, 1992.

38  P.B. Beaumont, *Human Resource Management: Key Concepts and Skills*, London, Sage, 1993, Chapter 1.

39  T.A. Kochan and P. Osterman, 'Human resource development and utilization: is there too little in the US?', mimeographed paper, Sloan School of Management, MIT, 1990, p. 33.

40  P.B. Beaumont, 'The diffusion of human resource management innovations', *Relations Industrielles*, 40 (2), 1985, pp. 243–56.

41  T.A. Kochan and L. Dyer, 'Managing transformational change: the role of human resource professionals', Sloan School of Management, MIT, Working Paper, April 1992.

42  D.K. Berlo et al., 'Dimensions for evaluating the acceptability of message sources', *Public Opinion Quarterly*, 33, 1969–70, pp. 563–76.

43  P.B. Beaumont and P.J.R. Richards, 'Inter-firm networks: seeking to sustain and diffuse QWL innovations', Report for ACAS Wales, 1993.

44  W.W. Daniel, 'Needed: a policy for industrial relations', *Policy Studies*, 11 (1), 1990, p. 26.

45  N. Millward, M. Stevens, D. Smart and W.R. Hawes, *Workplace Industrial Relations in Transition*, Aldershot, Dartmouth, 1992, pp. 264–6.

46  G. Smith, 'Employee share schemes in Britain', *Employment Gazette*, April 1993, pp. 149–54.

47  P.B. Beaumont and R.I.D. Harris, 'The pattern of diffusion of employee share ownership schemes in Britain: some key findings', mimeographed paper, 1994.

48  M. Poole, *The Origins of Economic Democracy: Profit Sharing and Employee Shareholding Schemes*, London, Routledge, 1989.

49  R.J. Long, 'The incidence and nature of employee profit sharing and share ownership in Canada', *Relations Industrielles*, 47 (Summer), 1992, pp. 463–88.

# 6
# COLLECTIVE BARGAINING AND THE FUTURE: AN EXTENDED OR CHANGED ROLE?

## INTRODUCTION

At the present time, collective bargaining still determines and regulates the terms and conditions of employment of a very sizeable minority of the total workforce in Britain; more particularly it remains the most important mechanism of union–management interaction in the public sector, and retains its strength in numerous private sector companies and establishments. Moreover, as employee–management conflicts are, at least to some extent, inherent in the employment relationship in hierarchical organizations, there will always be a need for some adjustment mechanism to deal with the distributive side of the employment relationship. For these reasons it would be inappropriate, not to say foolish, for collective bargaining not to figure prominently in any discussions about the future shape of the national industrial relations system.

However, the task facing collective bargaining, as it seeks to continue to play an important role in the national system, is a very considerable one. The nature of this task is illustrated by some estimates contained in a recent study which suggested that in the last five years or so some 60,000 employees were brought under new collective bargaining arrangements, but at the same time some 100,000 employees had ceased to be covered by such arrangements as a result of employer de-recognition initiatives.[1] In short, the difficult 'balancing act' facing the unions is to increase their presence and representation in the non-union sector, but via means that do not produce an employer backlash in the union sector that results in further (possibly greater) collective bargaining losses there. The expectation of further, and indeed enhanced, de-recognition initiatives in the years ahead suggests that this will be a far from straightforward exercise for the unions to accomplish.[2]

In seeking to accomplish this 'balancing act' the present chapter considers, firstly, the potential value of statutory union recognition provisions as a means of increasing the presence of collective bargaining in the non-union sector, and then, secondly, the case for bringing about a more integrative collective bargaining relationship that is more attractive to employers in both the union and non-union sectors of employment. However, before turning to these two matters it is useful to consider the changing nature of collective bargaining in recent years.

## CHANGING COLLECTIVE BARGAINING

In Chapter 1 it was observed that one of the chief claims made in favour of collective bargaining is its allegedly highly adaptive nature, in the sense of its ability and capacity to respond to the emergence of new demands, problems and circumstances. During the 1980s and into the 1990s product market and labour market circumstances very much tilted bargaining power in favour of employers. This was most obviously evidenced by the relatively low levels of strike activity in these years. As management were very much the pro-active agent of change in these years, it is important to consider what sort of demands they have made on the processes and outcomes of collective bargaining. That is, have they sought changes in the processes designed to establish more integrative, joint problem solving relationships, or have they concentrated mainly on bringing about substantive changes? The weight of available evidence (including the latter part of Chapter 4) tends to point towards more of an emphasis on the latter, with the particular concern being to produce outcomes that meet employer demands for increased flexibility of labour. This emphasis on substantive outcomes designed to facilitate the enhanced flexibility of labour has, of course, been very closely tied up with the increased decentralization of collective bargaining, which was discussed in Chapter 1.

A number of studies have documented the employer orientation along these lines. For instance, Ingram's work, based on the CBI wage data set for the manufacturing sector, indicated:

- In any one year throughout the 1980s, nearly 1 in 3 settlement groups that recognized a trade union introduced changes in working practices as part of the wage settlement.
- Over the decade as a whole, only 25 per cent of bargaining groups had not made any such changes in working practices, whereas over 50 per cent had made more than one such change.
- Changes in working practices tended to be associated with higher wage settlements and with a greater likelihood of industrial action.[3]

Some further research by Marsden and Thompson examined some 137 collective agreements for the period 1980–7 that contained flexibility clauses;[4] these covered some 7.5 per cent of the manufacturing workforce. Table 6.1 indicates that these flexibility clauses primarily concerned job demarcations and the deployment of labour within the plant or enterprise.

These collectively bargained changes in working practices, which were facilitated by higher wages and an increased (union) 'appreciation' of the realities of product market competition, were viewed as genuine changes that facilitated continuing changes in working *methods*, with the latter changes being of particular

Table 6.1  *Changes in working practices by main industrial sector, 1980–6*

| | Number of agreements mentioning these issues | | | | |
| Type of change | Engineering | Food and drink | Chemicals | Oil | Total |
|---|---|---|---|---|---|
| Working time | 10 | 1 | 4 | 1 | 16 |
| Part-time temporary | 3 | 1 | 0 | 0 | 4 |
| Subcontracting | 2 | 2 | 4 | 2 | 10 |
| Deployment | 37 | 7 | 5 | 11 | 60 |
| Skill demarcation | 23 | 6 | 8 | 4 | 41 |
| Grading | 20 | 4 | 3 | 1 | 28 |

*Source*: D. Marsden and M. Thompson, 'Flexibility agreements and their significance in the increase in productivity in British manufacturing since 1980', *Work, Employment and Society*, 4 (1), 1990, p. 90.

significance as a contribution to improved productivity. Furthermore, a recent comparison of the contents of some 100 collective agreements (in 50 companies) in the years 1979 and 1990 indicated (1) relatively little change in their procedural provisions, but (2) a great deal of change in their substantive provisions.[5] The latter involved the formalization of more flexible job descriptions, and even more noticeably the increased importance of management prerogative in determining job tasks. The theme of enhanced or reasserted managerial prerogative has been a strong theme in the literature in recent years.[6] Indeed, one study, which reported that the greatest productivity growth in 1988–9 occurred in companies where some de-recognition had occurred, interpreted this relationship in essentially these terms.[7]

In summary, it would appear that the substantive terms of collective bargaining have increasingly reflected management's priority demand for flexible working practices during the course of the 1980s. However, these substantive changes involved higher levels of wages, were associated with an increased likelihood of industrial action and were not noticeably underpinned by procedural changes that seemed to point towards the development of a more joint problem-solving collective bargaining approach. In short, the structures and outcomes of collective bargaining undoubtedly changed in the 1980s (and into the 1990s), but whether the underlying attitudes and patterns of behaviour did seems much more questionable.

If management have not taken the opportunity (when they very much had the ability to do so) to move in a joint problem-solving or partnership direction is this not their mistake, with the costs and adverse consequences falling very largely on them if in the future the political and economic environment should change and alter the balance of bargaining power in favour of unions? Certainly there are numerous arguments to the effect that the adversarial, arm's-length collective bargaining approach has involved costs for management; but what is much less common in the literature is any discussion of the potential costs and adverse implications for unions of the continued maintenance of an essentially adversarial collective bargaining approach. In fact if one looks at the 1980s experience in Britain there are at least two tendencies associated with the continued maintenance of relatively adversarial collective bargaining relationships that should be of some considerable concern to the unions.

1   Some of their apparent 'success' may not be an entirely unmixed blessing for them.
2   There are some apparently 'favourable circumstances' that they have not been able to translate into tangible gains.

The first proposition has to do with the size of the union-relative wage effect. The work of Blanchflower and Freeman has indicated that the size of the union-relative wage effect is much greater in the USA than in other countries, and that this has given US management 'an exceptional profit incentive to oppose unions, and is a major reason for US unionism declining more than for other countries'.[8] In other words, the size of the union-relative wage effect means that US members get the best wage return from their union dues, which should encourage increases in membership. But what has prevented this occurring, so the argument goes, is that this same effect produces an adverse management reaction which involves strong and sustained opposition to union organizing attempts.

Although well below that of the US, the size of the union-relative wage effect in Britain occupies about second place in a league table of such effects. Moreover, some existing research in Britain suggests that the size of this effect (around 10–11 per cent) remained essentially unchanged during the course of the 1980s.[9] To some commentators the maintenance of this effect through a very difficult decade may indicate the entrenched strength and resilience of unions and collective bargaining in Britain. A rather less sanguine interpretation would be that

● it can provide a justification for further anti-union legislation; and

● it can provide the stimulus for the maintenance (and arguably growth) of management opposition to unions in both the union and non-union employment sectors.

If traditional adversarial collective bargaining produces effects that will enhance or, at the very least, maintain the present level of employer opposition to it then clearly this will not make life easier for the unions in the future. At the same time, however, the unions have to offer some return for members' dues in order substantially to enhance their appeal to employees and their recruitment prospects in the non-union sector. In fact, in the 1980s (and into the 1990s) there were two sets of developments that would appear to have been favourable for unions in attracting new members, but that they have been unable to translate into actual membership gains. The first development involves a rise in the opinion poll ratings or public approval of unions as institutions. Table 6.2 presents some relevant information in this regard.

Table 6.2 indicates that during the 1980s, as union membership and collective bargaining coverage declined and strike levels fell to a record low, the public perceptions of unions as institutional entities became considerably more positive in nature. These findings and relationships are clearly at odds with a widely quoted paper that has argued that union growth is facilitated by increasingly favourable public perceptions of unions as worthwhile organizational entities.[10] Although the reasons for the increasingly favourable views of unions taken by the public at large remain a source of active debate and disagreement,[11] it is clear that the unions have not been able to realize any major tangible gains, such as increased membership, from the increasingly favourable trends observed in Table 6.2. The problem for the unions here may be that they face something in the way of an

Table 6.2   *Public opinion views of trade unions,
Britain, 1979–88 (%)*

|      | Trade unions are a good thing | Net popularity | Trade unions are too powerful |
|------|-------------------------------|----------------|-------------------------------|
| 1979 | 51 | 15 | 77 |
| 1980 | 60 | 31 | 70 |
| 1981 | 56 | 27 | 60 |
| 1982 | 59 | 29 | 63 |
| 1983 | 63 | 38 | 59 |
| 1984 | 60 | 30 | 64 |
| 1985 | 64 | 41 | 49 |
| 1986 | 67 | 45 | 45 |
| 1987 | 71 | 54 | 36 |
| 1988 | 68 | 57 | |

*Source*: D. Marsh, 'Public opinion, trade unions and Mrs Thatcher', *British Journal of Industrial Relations*, 28 (1), 1990, pp. 59–60.

inherent trade-off: membership growth occurs against a back-ground of increasingly unfavourable public views of them (for example, during the 1970s), whereas membership decline (and associated declines, such as in the level of strike activity) is associated with an increasingly favourable public view of them. If this is the case then the very circumstances that attract individual employees to join unions in numbers (namely, high levels of union activity) may produce an adverse impact on public opinions and perceptions, with the latter providing subsequent justification for anti-union legislative measures being introduced by a government committed to reducing union power.

The second development or occurrence that should have worked to the advantage of trade unions in the 1980s was an apparent rise in the levels of employee job dissatisfaction. As we saw in Chapter 3, it has long been argued, with considerable empirical support, that job dissatisfaction provides the critical trigger for employees to demand union representation. Admittedly we lack a large-scale, representative body of survey data that allows us to track job satisfaction trends over time (in Britain), but the following studies are worthy of note:

1   A fifteen-country study in the 1980s found that the UK respondents reported relatively low levels of satisfaction with the job as a whole, with various individual dimensions of the job, and with the management of the company.[12]
2   In the early 1990s a comparative study of employee satisfaction with various aspects of jobs in eight European countries placed Britain at the bottom of the league table in two successive years.[13]

The obvious question raised by findings of this kind is: why haven't the unions been able to capitalize on such levels of job dissatisfaction and substantially increase their membership and presence in the non-union employment sector? There are various possible explanations that can be put forward:

• Job dissatisfaction is disproportionately concentrated in the union, as opposed to the non-union, sector, which is an issue we addressed and explored in Chapter 3.
• The particular sources of job dissatisfaction are not the ones that unions are traditionally orientated to addressing.

- Unions committed to adversarial collective bargaining are not the particular adjustment mechanism favoured by employees.
- Unions have lacked the necessary information and resources to mount the levels of organizing activity that are required to capitalize on such job dissatisfaction.

Although all these may have played a role in failing to translate this dissatisfaction into new members, it is the last of them that is pursued in the next section. This particular concentration represents a further exploration of the reasons behind the observation made in Chapter 3 that many non-union organizations have been able to maintain their non-union status despite the relative absence of HRM practices as a 'union substitution' device.

## EXTENDING TRADITIONAL COLLECTIVE BARGAINING: A ROLE FOR STATUTORY PROCEDURES?

The three routes by which union recognition arrangements have historically been achieved in Britain have been by (i) discussion and negotiation, (ii) extension (that is, the recognition arrangements of existing plants in a multi-plant firm are automatically extended and applied to any new plants acquired or built) and (iii) voluntary conciliation involving a third party (for example, ACAS), with the first of these routes being the one most often used.[14] The question considered here is whether this discussion and negotiation route will be adequate from the union point of view in the future?

To extend traditional collective bargaining successfully into the non-union employment sector on a voluntary basis the unions will have to raise the priority that they have traditionally attached to the recruitment and organization of new members, and commit substantial organizational resources to provide tangible back-up to these initiatives. Furthermore, they will have to ensure that these recruitment initiatives are disproportionately concentrated in establishments where there is a relatively high probability of a successful outcome. That is, in sites where ideally (1) there is a substantial element of employee job dissatisfaction; (2) the particular source of this job dissatisfaction is known to the unions *before* they begin the organizing initiative; and (3) management opposition to a union presence is relatively limited. This is undoubtedly a tall order to achieve in a high-unemployment environment which means that, firstly, existing union members are likely to raise their servicing demands on unions (for example, in redundancy situations) and, secondly, that falling membership numbers are causing unions financial difficulties, which in turn lead to cutbacks in internal organizational resources.

Admittedly, the 1980s saw some individual unions launch a number of well-publicized recruitment drives that were concentrated in particular geographical locations, had a central organizing theme or were especially orientated towards particular categories of employees. However, the extent to which such campaigns were adequately resourced and capable of sustained maintenance over time and were cost-effective in terms of returns has been questioned.[15] Moreover, how representative such campaigns were of the general level of union organizing activity is also questionable in view of some survey findings which indicate that a substantial number of non-union employers had experienced no attempts to organize them.[16] The contents of Table 6.3 indicate the relatively conventional approaches to recruitment and recognition of three unions in recent years.

In Chapter 3 we argued that it was the limited extent of union organizing activities in the 1980s that was largely responsible for the limited inroads made into the non-union employment sector. This argument would appear to be borne out by Table 6.4. The message of the table seems to be that, unless *successful* union recruitment and recognition initiatives increased noticeably between 1979–83 and 1984–90 (which seems unlikely in view of the overall trend in union membership/recognition in these years), there is little obvious indication of increased union recruitment/recognition initiatives in the 1980s.

The organizational constraints on traditional union recruitment activities, enhanced management opposition to a union presence, and the falling union win rate in (ACAS) conciliated recognition claims (see Chapter 3) have all combined to produce a renewed union interest in having statutory union recognition provisions in Britain. At the 1987 Trades Union Congress one of the motions passed called for the future establishment of a legally enforceable threshold of trade union membership at individual workplaces, which would lead to automatic trade union recognition. And in

1991 the TUC produced a discussion document which suggested the following four-stage procedure.

Table 6.3  *Three union approaches to recruitment and recognition*

---

1  *The National Union of Knitwear, Footwear and Apparel Trades* (48,000 members)

- Eighty per cent of membership is associated with six national agreements.
- The union approaches an organization for recruitment facilities only when it employs around 100 workers.
- Recruitment difficulties are associated with high labour turnover and new small non-federated plants.
- Every six months a national officer reviews the (weekly) return figures of local officials, and a sizeable discrepancy between potential and actual membership will trigger a demand for a recruitment drive in a particular organization.

2  *The Furniture, Timber and Allied Trade Union* (35,000 members)

- A party to 26 national agreements, with federated firms being 'much easier to deal with'.
- Employer rejection (widespread) of an initial request for recruitment facilities leads to a factory-gate recruitment approach.
- A small core of 'activists' (with a prior history of trade union activity) is often crucial in selling the union to the rest of the workforce.
- The forthcoming merger with the GMB is expected to enhance the resources for recruitment.

3  *The National Communications Union* (150,000 members)

- Membership is overwhelmingly concentrated in BT.
- There is membership in some 100 communications companies, but recognition agreements in only 30 of these.
- The majority of cable companies (the fastest growing part of the sector) have opposed initial requests for recognition.
- Membership at Mercury Communications has risen from 80 to 800 in some 18 months, but there is no recognition agreement.[a]

---

[a] Mercury has agreed to meet the NCU to discuss the question of union recognition (*Financial Times*, 29 March 1994).

*Source*: Adapted from *IRS Employment Trends*, 550, December 1993.

Table 6.4    *Attempted union organizing rate (private sector only)*

| Period of time | Group of employees | Attempted recruitment | Attempted recognition |
| --- | --- | --- | --- |
| 1979–84 | Manual | 14.6% | 3.8% |
| 1984–90 | Manual | 10.5% | 4.4% |
| 1979–84 | Non-manual | 11.0% | 2.7% |
| 1984–90 | Non-manual | 9.2% | 3.8% |

These were unsuccessful union recruitment and recognition attempts at establishments remaining non-union at the end of the sub-period of time specified.

*Source*: P.B. Beaumont and R.I.D. Harris, 'The institutional vacuum in British industrial relations', *Policy Studies*, 15 (Winter), 1994.

1  *Representation* – any worker would have the right to be represented by a union in, for example, health and safety, maternity rights, equal pay and discrimination issues, even in the absence of any other union members in the workplace.

2  *Union facilities* – where the union had 10 per cent membership there would be a right for representatives to take time off work for union duties and training.

3  *Consultation* – a 20 per cent membership figure in a given bargaining unit would give the union the right to be consulted on issues such as the procedures for declaring redundancies.

4  *Negotiations* – would result from the unions demonstrating via a petition the existence of a membership level of 40 or 50 per cent.

Statutory recognition provisions have in fact operated in Britain in the years 1971–4 and 1976–80. Table 6.5 indicates some of the leading findings to emerge from the 1976–80 experience with such provisions. These findings, which parallel those for the earlier experience with statutory recognition provisions in 1971–4,[17] essentially reveal that union success in obtaining recognition arrangements was relatively limited. This was largely due to the existence of employer opposition, which was manifested in two different ways at two different stages of the procedure.

1 Employer opposition to white-collar employee recognition was concentrated at the conciliation and employee ballot stage, which resulted in a relatively long period of time being taken to hear and decide the claim.

2 Employer opposition to blue-collar employee recognition was concentrated at the post-ballot stage, being manifested in a relatively high level of non-compliance with the recommendation for recognition.

If statutory union recognition provisions are to be more successful (from the union point of view) in the future in Britain then these two problem areas and loopholes will have to be dealt

Table 6.5 *Statutory recognition provisions in Britain, 1976–80*

---

1 There were a total of 1,610 references, with the vast majority being settled at the initial conciliation stage.

2 Some 47.5 per cent of the settlements at the conciliation stage involved full or partial recognition.

3 Some 65 per cent of the 247 reports that went beyond the conciliation stage recommended full or partial recognition.

4 Only 53 per cent of the claims that went beyond the initial conciliation stage involving white-collar workers resulted in a recommendation for recognition, compared to 73 per cent of claims involving blue-collar workers. The lower win rate for white-collar claims was associated with strong employer opposition (as proxied by the length of time taken to hear and decide the claim) to recognition in relatively large-sized (average = 100 employees) bargaining units in multi-plant companies.

5 More than 50 per cent of the recommendations for recognition in claims that went beyond the initial conciliation stage were not complied with by employers. These were overwhelmingly the claims involving blue-collar workers in small-sized bargaining units (average = 36 employees) in single independent establishments, where the claim was settled relatively quickly, and with some two-thirds of employees voting in favour of union representation.

6 'Under the shadow' of the statutory procedures, the voluntary conciliation route to recognition was relatively well used, with a relatively high union win-rate resulting.

---

*Source*: P.B. Beaumont, 'Statutory recognition provisions in Britain, 1976–1980', *Relations Industrielles*, 38 (4), 1983, pp. 744–66.

with and closed. One country whose statutory recognition provisions may provide some useful guidelines and lessons in these regards is Canada, where (i) membership card counts, rather than employee ballots, provide the basis for recognition; (ii) there are relatively short, fixed time-periods for hearing and deciding recognition claims; and (iii) binding arbitration is provided for the first collective agreement following a recognition decision.[18] However, in designing legislation to address the above problem areas it will be important to ensure that the relevant third party body responsible for operating these arrangements does not experience a level of operational difficulties that can be seized upon by a Government as a reason for repealing such provisions; this was, of course, what happened in the 1976–80 period.

It is difficult to envisage collective bargaining arrangements penetrating the non-union employment sector in the future, at least to any substantial degree, in the absence of statutory recognition procedures. This being said, the following associated points should be borne in mind:

- Statutory recognition procedures may have to involve a quid pro quo, namely statutory de-recognition procedures.
- Procedures that appear to be slanted in the unions' favour will generate an employer search for loopholes and may produce an employer backlash against unions that may not augur well for the longer-term maintenance of the procedures.
- Highly legislative and adversarial procedures will pose operational difficulties for the responsible administrative bodies, and will risk the creation of adversarial collective bargaining relationships from the outset.
- The fit of statutory recognition procedures with other possible legislation (for example, works councils) will have to be carefully considered.

## SEEKING TO CHANGE COLLECTIVE BARGAINING

If collective bargaining is to play a significant role in filling the existing institutional vacuum in the system it will not be sufficient simply to extend traditional collective bargaining arrangements via statutory procedures. At the same time it will be necessary to try to move collective bargaining in more of a joint problem-solving, less adversarial direction. A move in this direction, for example, would arguably lessen employer opposition to union recognition and involve collective bargaining more centrally in the continuing process of the introduction of HRM practices orientated towards individual employees.

Advocates of a move along these lines invariably highlight the need for more trust, openness and communication between unions and management on a regular, on-going basis. However, it is important to look behind these very general terms with a view to identifying some of the leading factors that can help bring them about. A review of the existing literature highlights the potential relevance and importance of the following factors.[19]

1 The existence of certain competitiveness difficulties in the product market that necessitate a change of existing attitudes and behaviours, most notably the development of the view that such problems must be tackled jointly.

2 A change of leading personalities on both the union and management sides, with the newcomers being much more well-disposed towards a joint problem-solving approach.

3 The successful conduct of programmes of attitude-change by third parties in union–management relationships characterized by a tradition of adversarial dealings. In Britain there have been joint working parties established by ACAS for such purposes, while in the US there has been a 'relations by objectives' programme operated by the FMCS and experiments in 'win–win' or mutual gains bargaining.

4 A management willingness to take the initiative in this direction in its dealings with the unions, because it (a) recognizes the inevitability of having to operate in a relatively highly unionized situation and/or (b) is seeking to change its competitive strategy in a 'more added value' direction, which necessitates more priority being attached to the employment–management relationship.

As an illustration of the influence of some of these factors, the next section presents some key findings deriving from a recent study of industrial relations in the paper and board industry in the UK.[20]

## THE PAPER AND BOARD INDUSTRY: A JOINT PROBLEM-SOLVING APPROACH

The paper and board industry in the UK has faced strong, sustained and successful foreign competition in recent decades. This has resulted in a major restructuring of the industry, as indicated by the following figures:

- The number of federated paper mills has fallen from 146 in 1972 to 84 in 1992.

- The number of paper machines in federated establishments has declined from 410 in 1972 to 168 in 1992.

- The total number of employees (manual and staff) in federated mills has fallen from 63,038 in 1972 to 24,917 in 1992.

As well as the industry becoming much smaller-sized, its the pattern of ownership has also changed noticeably. For instance, there has been the growth of foreign investment, with currently nearly two-thirds of the industry being foreign-owned. An associated change is the fact that nearly all major production units in the UK are exclusively or largely owned by specialist paper-making organizations. This position contrasts sharply with the 1970s when many of the mills were family-owned or owned by large, conglomerate companies that were not exclusively or even primarily paper-makers.

This combination of downsizing and changing ownership has, according to many industry specialists, been associated with increased reinvestment in the industry, an accelerated pace of technical change, the growth of a more professional management, and changes in the competitive strategy of the industry. This last has involved for example individual mills reducing the size of their product range and either concentrating on high-volume, bulk-grade production or adopting a more specialist, niche-marketing orientation.

These changes, in turn, have resulted in an improvement in various measures of industry performance in the 1980s and into the 1990s. The following figures are of note here:

1   Production of paper in the UK rose from 3,197,600 tons in 1982 to 5,128,000 tons in 1992; the improved production position in the newsprint sub-sector was particularly notable in these years.

2 Consumption of paper in the UK rose from 6.8 million tons in 1982 to 9.6 million tons in 1992.

3 The volume of exports rose from 397,000 tons in 1982 to 1,519,100 tons in 1992.

4 Wages per manual employee rose by 110.3 per cent in the period 1983–92, whereas production per employee rose by 123.2 per cent and wages per ton of production actually fell by 5.4 per cent in these years.

The above should not obscure the existence of continuing difficulties and concerns in the industry at the present time. For instance, the adverse trade balance in paper and board remains sizeable, imports still account for around 60 per cent of UK consumption of paper and board, and the extent of price-cutting in the early 1990s recession has been a major source of concern.

In industrial relations terms the paper and board industry in the UK has historically been characterized by (1) a relatively high level of union organization among manual workers and (2) well-established industry or national-level bargaining arrangements. Have these traditional industrial relations features of the industry survived the extensive restructuring process indicated above? And if they have survived, have they inhibited or facilitated production and working practices changes at the individual mill level?

Looking at these traditional industrial relations features in turn, Table 6.6 sets out the unionization figures for manual employees in federated mills for various years since 1976. It indicates that the level of union organization among manual employees has remained remarkably stable in the face of the major restructuring which has occurred in the industry. This relatively high level of union organization, which has been underpinned by the national agreement, has arguably facilitated organizational change at the individual mill level. This is because trade unions are more likely to co-operate with management in the process of organizational change if their institutional presence and role is not being strongly threatened or undermined. As one personnel director in the industry put it: 'The unions, looking at these figures, could only conclude that we had made no attempt to undermine them, or else we had done a very poor job of it.'

Turning now to the place and role of national bargaining, the following preliminary points should be noted:

Table 6.6    *Union density, (manual workers only), in the paper and board industry (federated establishments only), various years*

|      | Manual worker union density (%) |
| ---- | :---: |
| 1976 | 91 |
| 1983 | 92 |
| 1987 | 91 |
| 1990 | 87 |
| 1993 | 86 |

The level of union density among staff employees (not covered by national bargaining arrangements) has also been relatively stable in these years, albeit at a much lower overall level:  the relevant figures here are 32% (1976), 38% (1983), 29% (1987), 37% (1990) and 34% (1993).

*Source*: Figures supplied by the Paper Federation of Great Britain.

1    Supplementary bargaining at the individual mill level is a relatively long-standing feature of the industry. The New Earnings Survey for 1978, for instance, indicated that some 71.7 per cent of male manual employees in the industry were affected by a supplementary agreement.

2    The membership of the industry federation has declined over time (109 members in 1976 to 62 in 1992) as closures have occurred, but the larger-sized organizations (with the exception of the tissues sub-sector) have very much stayed with the federation. As a result the federation membership currently accounts for some 86 per cent of mills and 90 per cent of production in the industry.

The national agreement is very much a minimum-wage-rate agreement, but has been important in providing an enabling framework and set of guidelines for non-wage changes in the industry. The 1982 national agreement, for instance, was the first industry-level agreement in the UK to facilitate the introduction of annual-hours working arrangements. Table 6.7 indicates the extent of the movement in this direction in the industry over the course

Table 6.7 *Annual hours developments in the paper and board industry post-1982*

|  | % of mills on annual hours | % of manual employees working annual hours |
| --- | --- | --- |
| 1983 | 2.7 | 6.7 |
| 1984 | 4.7 | 9.1 |
| 1985 | 14.5 | 23.8 |
| 1986 | 16.5 | 25.3 |
| 1987 | 23.4 | 36.9 |
| 1988 | 25.2 | 35.9 |
| 1989 | 32.1 | 42.7 |
| 1990 | 33.0 | 41.0 |
| 1991 | 43.0 | 51.6 |
| 1992 | 48.5 | 57.7 |
| 1993 | 52.4 | 67.4 |

*Source*: Figures supplied by the Paper Federation of Great Britain.

of time. This is, firstly, an important illustrative example of how national bargaining can assist organizational change at the individual establishment. That is, in keeping with the inter-systems diffusion findings discussed in Chapter 5, national-level bargaining can assist the diffusion process by providing sponsorship for a particular organizational innovation, helping build a consensus as to its potential worth and spreading information concerning its performance value and 'pay-off' – on the latter point, the employment affairs department of the federation has been a major source of technical advice and assistance to member companies seeking to move in the annual-hours direction. Secondly, the unions have been extensively involved in discussions, consultations and negotiations at the individual mill level that have filled in the local-level details concerning annual-hours working arrangements. Thirdly, the movement to annual-hours working arrangements has been accompanied by a sharp rise in the level of workforce training, with again union representatives being prominently represented in decision-making circles. The training body for the industry operates on a tripartite basis (with five representatives appointed by the unions), with particular emphasis being currently placed on the development of multi-skilled craft workers to increase employee flexibility, reduce response time to breakdowns, reduce machine and equipment downtime and reduce the use of outside contractors. More than a third of the federated mills are currently involved in multi-skilled training programmes, with the industry sub-committee overseeing these developments being chaired by a union official.

It is also apparent that various measures of industrial conflict have declined in the industry in recent years. Table 6.8 presents some relevant information in this regard. The strong downwards

Table 6.8    *Measures of dispute activity in the paper and board industry (federated establishments), 1972–92*

|      | Strikes | Conferences[a] |
|------|---------|----------------|
| 1972 | 12 | 74 |
| 1973 | 31 | 89 |
| 1974 | 34 | 127 |
| 1975 | 7 | 107 |
| 1976 | 13 | 78 |
| 1977 | 17 | 96 |
| 1978 | 24 | 116 |
| 1979 | 22 | 117 |
| 1980 | 5 | 104 |
| 1981 | 6 | 59 |
| 1982 | 5 | 61 |
| 1983 | 5 | 42 |
| 1984 | 12 | 50 |
| 1985 | 1 | 43 |
| 1986 | 4 | 48 |
| 1987 | 2 | 43 |
| 1988 | 1 | 38 |
| 1989 | 4 | 58 |
| 1990 | 1 | 29 |
| 1991 | 0 | 29 |
| 1992 | 1 | 30 |

[a] These are procedural meetings (which may occur at the mill or national levels) convened to resolve union–management disputes.

*Source*: Information provided by the Paper Federation of Great Britain.

trend in these figures is clearly not inconsistent with the basic proposition that a considerable element of union–management co-operation characterizes the paper and board industry at the present time. However, to establish such a proposition more clearly one needs to move beyond such figures, because of their well-known limitations for drawing any firm conclusions about the overall quality of union–management relationships: such figures are not a complete measure of all forms of industrial conflict; the absence of conflict does not necessarily indicate a co-operative joint problem-solving relationship between unions and management; and such indices of conflict have fallen across a wide range of industries, and it is highly questionable, to say the least, to conclude that this indicates a widespread level of union–management co-operation throughout British industry.

Accordingly, to pursue the matter further we conducted a series of interviews with human resources managers in more than 10 per cent of all UK paper mills. In Box 6.1 is to be found a set of brief snapshots of six such mills. The major impressions and findings to emerge from these management interviews were as follows:

- A great deal of attention was being given to the task of reformulating or reinforcing the nature of their competitive strategy. The obtaining of BS 5750 accreditation and moves in the TQM direction were particularly prominent in this regard.

- Functional flexibility changes involving tighter manning levels, broader job descriptions, enhanced workforce training (particularly multi-skill and cross-training), annual-hours working arrangements and operator responsibility for quality, etc., were very much in evidence; these were frequently accompanied by technological changes.

- High levels of union density (among manual employees) were apparent, with good, co-operative union–management relationships being widely reported.

- New initiatives to enhance employee involvement (via communication or group working) were widespread, although these were never viewed as an alternative to, or substitute for, communication, discussion and consultation with union representatives.

**Box 6.1   *Six illustrative examples from the paper and board industry***

1   This mill, which is in the printings and writings sub-sector of the industry, currently has some 600 employees, a figure down from around 1,200 five years ago. It is a member of the Federation, but supplements the nationally agreed rates with local bargaining. As redundancies have occurred over time, local bargaining has been the route through which increasingly flexible working arrangements have been established; this has involved an expansion of technical skills training. In an attempt to reduce delivery times to customers further (already down from three weeks two years ago to ten days currently) as a central plank in its service-orientated competitive strategy, the mill has recently introduced a TQM training programme. This programme is deliberately proceeding slowly (being confined at present to managerial personnel), as the unions have expressed some initial scepticism about TQM, and the management is keen not to risk disrupting the co-operative union–management relationship which exists (union density among manuals is virtually 100 per cent).

2   This mill, which is in the case materials sub-sector of the industry, currently has some 180 employees, a figure down from 250 seven years ago. It is a member of the Federation, with local bargaining only (for the last five years or so) covering bonus payment matters. The reduced employment numbers have been associated with tighter manning levels, broader job descriptions and skill extension. Following BS 5750 accreditation, the mill is seeking to expand its foreign customer base, and to this end is currently exploring the potential value of TQM. These developments have been associated with an extensive set of communications initiatives (for example employee attitudes surveys; written and verbal briefings) designed to maintain the good working relationship between unions and management (union density among manuals is virtually 100 per cent).

3   This greenfield-site operation established in the mid-1980s is in the newsprint sub-sector of the industry. It is a high-volume, low-cost producer, based on state-of-the-art

Box 6.1 *continued*

technology. A single-union recognition agreement (there is currently 80 per cent unionization on the shop floor), which involves a no status quo clause, flexible work operations (no individual job descriptions; only four main grades of labour), and single-status terms and conditions, has operated from the inception of the mill. It is a non-participating member of the Federation (that is, it is not party to the national agreed terms and conditions)* that currently has a workforce of 493, a figure up from 250 at the start-up time. It has recently introduced a profit-sharing scheme and private medical insurance, and initiated a set of problem-solving groups (designed to pave the way towards full team working), and holds quarterly meetings with union representatives and employees to share information on performance, plans and prospects. The union–management relationship is viewed as a relatively co-operative one.

4   This mill, which is in the packaging boards sub-sector of the industry, currently has some 400 employees, a figure down from around 550 six years ago. It is a member of the Federation which does not engage in local, supplementary bargaining. A traditional high-volume producer, it has sought to increase export sales in the last five years or so through a strong quality emphasis which has involved BS 5750 accreditation and the introduction of a TQM programme. The latter has been associated with an extensive training programme (including a multi-skilling exercise on the engineering side), the carrying out of a number of employee attitude surveys, the introduction of team briefing arrangements, and the establishment of quality-improvement teams. There has also been a substantial investment in new technology and the movement to annual-hours arrangements. Union density is virtually 100 per cent on the shop floor, with a good, co-operative union–management relationship being reported.

5   This mill, which is in the printings and writings sub-sector of the industry, currently has 650 employees, a figure down from some 750 five years go. It is a member of the Federation, but engages in local, supplementary bargaining every second year. It is a high-value-added producer, in which BS 5750 accreditation has been followed first by a TQM programme and currently by a customer-focus one. Technical change, broader job descriptions for senior operators, multi-skill training on the

Box 6.1 *continued*

engineering side, TQM training and a new health and safety programme have been major initiatives in the last five years or so. The current move to annual-hours operation has involved discussions with the workforce and the unions over an 18-month period, as the management are keen to 'carry all employees with them' (union density among manuals is virtually 100 per cent).

6    This mill, which is in the printings and writings sub-sector of the industry, currently has some 550 employees, a figure up from 450 five years ago. It is a member of the Federation, but with local supplementary bargaining occurring. It has a mixed competitive strategy, involving both high-volume/low-cost production and production for the high-value-added end of the market. It has moved to semi-continuous work operations, with an accompanying no compulsory redundancy pledge, has harmonized all major terms and conditions of employment (with the exception of sick pay) in the last ten years or so, has introduced a number of new communication measures (for example team briefing in 1987), has operated a profit-sharing scheme for twelve years and is currently discussing with the workforce and unions a proposal to introduce a profit-related pay element (union density among manuals is essentially 100 per cent).

* This rule change was introduced by the Federation in 1982. Currently some twelve companies (mainly greenfield-site operations) are in this category.

- Long-standing union–management discussion forums remained in place, and were increasingly supplemented by special meetings with union representatives.
- The scope or subject range of local (mill-level) bargaining was tending to widen over time.

To supplement this information, personal and telephone interviews were conducted with union officials in all parts of the country in which there was a reasonably sizeable concentration of paper mills. There were a number of important individual points to emerge from the union interviews, but the all-important general theme to emphasize here was the high degree of convergence between union and management views. That is, both sets of respondents saw substantial organizational change at the individual mill level which had been very much facilitated by a joint problem-solving union–management relationship. Box 6.2 contains an extract from a letter received from a leading national union officer in the industry.

In the last section we listed some of the factors and influences that commentators have suggested can help move a union–management relationship in the joint problem-solving direction. Which of these were most influential in the particular case of the paper and board industry? The major ones seemed to be as follows:

1 the competitive problems facing the industry, which stimulated the need for change;
2 management acceptance of the inevitability of dealing with unions given the industry tradition of high union organization and the national procedural agreement that underpinned this organization; and
3 the shift in competitive strategy to more of a product quality emphasis, which raised the priority attached to employment–

---

**Box 6.2  *Letter from a national union officer in the paper and board industry***

Although the relationship was good in the 1970s there has been a steady progress in the quality of the union–management relationship in the paper industry throughout the 1980s and into the 1990s. The leading factors responsible for bringing about this good quality relationship are the improved involvement and communication within the mills and the improved grievances and disputes procedures which have been very effective. Another major reason, I would suggest, is that following the drastic reductions and closures of the 1970s and early 1980s there has been more of a sense of 'pulling together' to fight off the competition, and in some cases, to avoid closure. This has led to a better realization and understanding of the industry as a whole.

management issues and considerations. As one managing director in the industry succinctly, not to say graphically, put it: 'Going down the quality improvement route we have to carry the unions and employees with us, or we're f—'.

To these factors I would attach two particular embellishments:

- The nature of the industry response (including enhanced union–management co-operation) to tough product market competition has been 'rewarded' (and hence reinforced) by improved performance, although the pressure remains to keep the response going.
- The national procedural/recognition agreement (which has underpinned union density in the industry) gives *tangible* expression to the trust and social belief systems (concerning the legitimacy of the other party) of the leading union and management representatives, which Walton and McKersie have identified as being of critical importance in shaping a co-operative attitudinal structuring process.[21] Moreover, these procedures ensure that the attitudes that they encapsulate can survive the turnover of key individuals in the industry.

The maintenance of national bargaining arrangements and a high level of union density at the present time clearly indicate that we have been discussing a rather atypical industry. This being said, the purpose of the discussion was to highlight some of the factors that can contribute to the creation and maintenance of a less adversarial collective bargaining relationship. In this sense the lessons to be drawn from the paper industry should not be seen as unique to that industry.

## SUMMARY

This chapter has concentrated on collective bargaining as a mechanism that can, will and should figure in any discussions concerning the future shape of the British industrial relations system. Although collective bargaining continues to decline it still remains important in many industries, companies and plants; indeed the General Secretary of the TUC has recently noted that 47 out of Britain's 50 most profitable companies recognize unions

(*Daily Telegraph*, 2 March 1994). The major points that have been made in the course of this chapter are:

- Increased employer demands for flexibility have translated into working practice changes being attached to wage increases, although rather less attention seems to have been given to the procedural side of the relationship.
- Statutory recognition provisions will be essential to increase the union presence in the non-union sector, although earlier problems with such provisions will have to be corrected.
- Extending the coverage of collective bargaining by statutory recognition provisions will need to be accompanied by initiatives designed to produce more of a joint problem-solving orientation in union–management relations.

## REFERENCES

1  *IRS Employment Trends*, 545, October, 1993.
2  *IRS Employment Trends*, 549, November, 1993.
3  P.N. Ingram, 'Changes in working practices in British manufacturing industry in the 1980s: a study of employee concessions made during wage negotiations', *British Journal of Industrial Relations*, 29 (1), 1991, pp. 1–14.
4  D. Marsden and M. Thompson, 'Flexibility agreements and their significance in the increase in productivity in British manufacturing since 1980', *Work, Employment and Society*, 4 (1), 1990, pp. 83–104.
5  Cited in D. Metcalf, 'Transformation of British industrial relations? Institutions, conduct and outcomes 1980–1990', Centre for Economic Performance, LSE, Discussion Paper 151, 1993, p. 10.
6  J. Purcell, 'The rediscovery of management prerogative: the management of labour relations in the 1980s', *Oxford Review of Economic Policy*, 7 (March), 1991, pp. 33–43.
7  P. Gregg, S. Machin and D. Metcalf, 'Signals and cycles? Productivity growth and changes in union status in British companies 1984–9', *Economic Journal*, 103, September 1993, pp. 894–907.
8  D.G. Blanchflower and R.B. Freeman, 'Unionism in the United States and other advanced OECD countries', *Industrial Relations*, 31 (1), 1992, pp. 62–3.
9  A. Oswald, 'Pay setting, self-employment and the unions: themes of the 1980s', *Oxford Review of Economic Policy*, 7, 1992.

10  S.M. Lipset, 'Labor unions in the public mind', in S.M. Lipset (ed.), 1986, *Unions in Transition*, San Francisco, ICS Press, 1986, pp. 287–322.

11  R. Richardson, 'Public opinion towards trade unions in Great Britain 1954–92', Centre for Economic Performance, LSE, Working Paper 504, 1993.

12  G.W. England, 'Worker satisfaction', in F. Adler et al. (eds), *Automation and Industrial Workers, Vol. 2, Part 1*, Oxford, Pergamon Press, pp. 147–91.

13  *Industrial Relations Review and Report*, 510, 1992; *Financial Times*, 2 February 1994.

14  P.B. Beaumont and B. Towers, 'Approaches to trade union recognition', in B. Towers (ed.), *A Handbook of Industrial Relations Practice*, 3rd edn, London, Kogan Page, 1992, pp. 123–36.

15  P.B. Beaumont and R.I.D. Harris, 'Union recruitment and organising attempts in Britain in the 1980s', *Industrial Relations Journal*, 21 (4), 1990, pp. 274–86.

16  TUC, *Organising for the 1990s*, London, TUC, 1989, p. 26.

17  B. James, 'Third party intervention in recognition disputes: the role of the Commission on Industrial Relations', *Industrial Relations Journal*, 8, 1977.

18  Beaumont and Towers, 'Approaches', in Towers (ed.), *Handbook of Industrial Relations Practice*, 3rd edn, pp. 130–2.

19  See, for example, J. Purcell, *Good Industrial Relations*, London, Macmillan, 1981. Also T.A. Kochan, H.C. Katz and R.B. McKersie, *The Transformation of American Industrial Relations*, New York, Basic Books, 1986.

20  P.B. Beaumont and L.C. Hunter, 'Industrial restructuring: the case of the paper and board industry', mimeographed paper, University of Glasgow, 1994.

21  R.E. Walton and R.B. McKersie, *A Behavioural Theory of Labor Negotiations*, New York, McGraw Hill, 1965, Chapter 6.

# 7

# LEARNING FROM ABROAD: WORKS COUNCILS IN GERMANY

## INTRODUCTION

At the risk of stating the obvious there is currently a great deal of interest in the future shape of the British industrial relations system. For example, in 1993 the House of Commons Employment Committee launched an enquiry into the future role of trade unions, and how unions can best fulfil that role. Various unions, companies and employer bodies provided evidence to the committee, with some of the leading points made being as follows:

- Unions saw the collective bargaining relationship as remaining important, but stressed that 'new' items such as training and equal opportunities must be increasingly on the bargaining agenda.
- Employers were more ambivalent about the future strength of collective bargaining, frequently suggesting that individual employee-centred HRM practices were now viewed as a more important route to organizational effectiveness.
- The unions favoured the establishment of statutory recognition provisions, saw the provision of protection, support and advice to individual members as being important now and in the future, and noted the growth of a wider range of consumer services to members (for example credit cards, discounted mortgages).
- The importance of the external lobbying role of unions was also frequently noted.[1]

Perhaps the safest conclusion to reach from the above is that an increasingly diverse set of arrangements will characterize the British industrial relations system in the future (elements such as individual representation by unions, conventional collective bargaining, HRM practices), with arguably the chief points of controversy being (1) whether HRM practices will increasingly complement (or substitute for) collective bargaining relationships in the unionized sector, and (2) whether unions can (and on what basis?) increasingly penetrate the non-union employment sector.

The potential for an even more diverse system in the future was provided when the 1991 meeting of the TUC carried a resolution calling for an examination of 'how features of the Franco-German approach to industrial relations – such as works councils and greater rights to information and consultation – might be adapted to British circumstances and traditions'. This was followed by a TUC study visit in 1992 to investigate the operation of works councils in Germany, and to assess their potential for adoption in Britain.[2] British unions' current interest in works council arrangements is a sharp departure from their historical position, which clearly reflects their concern about the declining role of collective bargaining.

The approach of the TUC goes to the heart of what some commentators have viewed as the essence of international industrial relations:[3] that is, what are the relevant lessons of experience abroad with a particular institutional arrangement, and can any positive lessons be successfully transplanted elsewhere? The French and German systems have two different works council models: the German model involves employee representatives only, whereas the French model is a joint management–employee representative body. In this particular chapter we concentrate solely on the German model, in view of the TUC concentration on it and also because rather more research-based material concerning its operation and performance (at least in English) exists. This concentration should not, however, preclude future examination and discussion of the relevance of the French model to possible adoption in Britain.

## SOME PRELIMINARY VIEWS CONCERNING WORKS COUNCILS

The West German system of industrial relations was considered the model system for others to emulate in the 1970s. However, in that decade attention focused overwhelmingly on worker directors on company boards, rather than on works councils. Indeed, in the 1970s worker directors were viewed as the essence of 'industrial democracy' in Europe, with some eight European countries passing legislation to introduce worker directors for the first time, or to strengthen already existing legislation in the matter, in the years 1970–9.[4] Indeed, until the 1980s there seemed to be a view in many countries – certainly in Britain – that works councils were a rather less highly developed form of institutional arrangements than collective bargaining. A fairly typical view along these lines came from Kendall, who highlighted the following 'limitations' on the role of the works council in West Germany:

- It cannot invoke economic sanctions against an employer.
- It is dependent on the employer for finance and facilities.
- It has limited information and expertise to challenge the employer's viewpoint and proposals.
- It can easily be steered by an employer to focus on non-strategic issues.[5]

This sort of view often went a stage further, to argue that the performance of works councils was highly variable in nature, with only those councils whose membership contained a relatively high proportion of union members being active and effective employee-representation bodies. Furthermore, there has been a relatively long-standing concern in union circles both within and outside Germany about the problems of dual representation arrangements. An ILO study in the early 1970s, for example, made the following observations:

> The balance between trade unions and works councils has never been a perfectly stable one, but until quite recently the existing statutory and *de facto* division of labour appeared to be the optimum solution to the problem of what in effect amounted to dual representation of employee interests. In the past few years, however, a number of developments have occurred that call into question the continuation of this long maintained equilibrium.[6]

The developments referred to above involved (1) the growth of union organization at the plant level and (2) works councils moving into subject areas that were close to those covered by collective bargaining arrangements at the industry/regional level. The essence of the dual representation concern from the union point of view is that individual employees value and identify more closely with works councils (which are not solely union representation bodies) in the plant than with the unions and collective bargaining at the industry level. Table 7.1 indicates some substantive support for this sort of concern.

At the present time, advocates of the case for adopting works councils in Britain are likely to make the following sorts of points in favour of the institution.

- They can represent the whole of the workforce, including manual and non-manual employees, and union and non-union employees.
- They can promote co-operative relationships within the organization.
- Their broad-ranging agenda can cover strategic level matters as well as issues pertaining to both individual employees and groups of employees.

Table 7.1   *Employee views of unions and works councils: a West German sample*

| Statement | Union (mean score) | Works council (mean score) |
|---|---|---|
| 1  This institution is essential in representing worker interests. | 4.25 | 4.47 |
| 2  This institution has done a lot to help workers in my company. | 3.91 | 4.13 |
| 3  To better promote worker interests, it would be a good idea to increase the power of this institution. | 3.72 | 4.18 |

This sample involves 135 individuals in 5 firms in the auto and metal industries.

*Source*: C.J. Hobson and J.B. Dworkin, 'West German labour unrest: are unions losing out to works councils?', *Monthly Labor Review*, 109 (2), 1986, p. 48.

These sorts of 'pluses' for the institution very much derive from experience in Germany, which we examine in the next section.

## WORKS COUNCILS IN GERMANY

Works councils in Germany have a relatively long history, stretching back into the nineteenth century. They were first put on a statutory basis in 1920, although in the 1920s and 1930s many workplaces lacked them, and those that existed were frequently caught up in relatively adversarial employee–management relations.[7] The present arrangements derive from legislation in 1952, although important subsequent amendments occurred in 1972, 1976 and 1988.[8] Some of the leading characteristics of works councils in Germany are as follows:

- They are mandatory in companies with more than 5 employees.
- The number of (exclusively) employee representatives increases with the level of employment up to 31 in companies with 9,000 employees.
- Company works councils may be established in multi-plant enterprises and group works councils in groups of companies.
- Blue-collar and white-collar employees can submit separate lists of candidates, although in practice joint lists are common.
- All employees aged 18 or more are entitled to vote for candidates.
- Seats are allocated on the basis of proportional representation.
- There is special provision to ensure the protection of white-collar interests.
- The Labour Court settles any disputes concerning elections.

Works councils have extensive rights as regards information, consultation and co-determination. Table 7.2 lists some of the leading rights covered under these headings.

It is important at this stage to emphasize or re-emphasize that (1) collective bargaining is conducted at the industry/regional levels in Germany; (2) works councils cannot invoke industrial

Table 7.2   *Some leading rights of works councils in (West) Germany*

---

1   *Information*

- Employers have to provide information concerning manpower planning, the introduction of new technology and working processes.

- In firms with more than 100 employees an economic committee (selected by the works council) has to be established and informed on a range of economic and financial matters, such as production levels, sales, investment, profits, rationalization plans and changes in work organization.

- Works councils in all firms with more than 20 employees must receive information on matters such as the introduction of new working methods, closures and transfers.

2   *Consultation*

- The employer has a duty to consult (before taking any action) with works councils on work organization changes.

- In firms with more than 20 employees works councils have the right to demand compensation for any proposed changes (such as sizeable redundancies, plant rundowns and changes in work organization) likely substantially to disadvantage employee interests. The parties seek to agree a 'social plan' in this regard, which can involve seeking the assistance of an independent conciliation board.

- Consultation must occur over individual and collective dismissals.

3   *Co-determination*

- Full rights apply in areas such as pay procedures, the organization of working time, health and safety measures, the fixing of bonus rates, etc.

- Wages and working conditions settled by collective agreements at the industry/regional levels cannot be the subject of works-level agreements unless the relevant collective agreement authorizes supplementary bargaining (this has occurred in relation to bonuses and job evaluation schemes).

- The works council has consent rights in matters concerning the recruitment, grading and transfer of personnel in firms with more than 20 employees.

---

*Source*: Based on J.T. Addison, K. Kraft and J. Wagner, 'German works councils and firm performance', in B.E. Kaufman and M.M. Kleiner (eds), *Employee Representation: Alternatives and Future Directions*, IRRA, Madison, University of Wisconsin, 1993, pp. 307–9.

action against employers; and (3) the majority of works council members are union members. This last point requires some elaboration. In the 1987 elections some 72 per cent of works councillors were union members,[9] a figure that may be compared to the overall union density figure of 35–6 per cent at that time.[10] However, it is worth noting that:

- The non-union membership proportion of works councils has shown some tendency to increase over time.[11]

- The non-union proportion among both blue- and white-collar employees is higher in smaller-sized firms, and in service sector industries.[12]

## VIEWS AND ASSESSMENTS OF THE GERMAN WORKS COUNCILS

The operation of works council arrangements in Germany has been assessed from various points of view (employees, management), and using a variety of research methods, although qualitative interviews and case studies have been the predominant approach. For instance, the contents of Table 7.1, although based on a small sample, suggest that employees attach more priority to works councils than to unions in representing their views and interests in the workplace. Secondly, a number of interview-based studies (again admittedly with small samples) of managers indicate relatively favourable views of works councils.[13] Typically such studies have suggested that (1) management views works councils as involving costs, particularly as regards slowing down the pace of decision-making processes, but (2) such costs are outweighed by the benefits of the arrangements in facilitating better-quality management decisions (necessitated by the need for forward planning) and more effective implementation of decisions (through the council's facilitating communication with the workforce). The sort of response which has emerged from research along these lines is indicated by the following comment from a manager in a US-owned auto facility in Germany:

> There are three major advantages of councils. First you're forced to consider in your decision-making process the effect on the employees in advance ... This avoids costly mistakes. Second, works councils will in the final run support the company. They will take into account the pressing needs of the company more than a trade

union can, on the outside. And third, works councils explain and defend certain decisions of the company toward the employees. Once decisions are made, they are easier to implement.[14]

The qualitative assessments such as this have been supplemented with some (admittedly still limited) quantitative research concerning the performance of works councils in Germany. The latter work has been primarily concerned to assess whether works councils are positively or negatively associated with various measures of a firm's organizational and economic performance; essentially the monopoly vs voice/responsive faces of unionism approach (see Chapter 1) has been applied to works councils. The available research is relatively inconclusive in nature, in the sense that neither strong positive nor negative performance relationships are observed.[15] This has meant that advocates of works councils can claim that such arrangements are not a drag on economic performance, whereas critics can emphasize that such arrangements do not appear to enhance performance.

The major limitation of this quantitative work is that it simply uses the presence (or not) of a works council as a variable in the estimating equations. That is, works councils (where present) are treated as essentially homogeneous in nature, with no attempt being made to measure or assess variation in the composition and activities of the councils. This is a major omission in research on works councils in Germany, where much more attention needs to be given to the heterogeneity of works councils. In other words, one should recognize that not all works councils are alike, and that research should concentrate on (1) identifying the key dimensions or lines along which such variation occurs and (2) seeking to identify the factors that account for this variation. This would be a logical and much-needed extension to some qualitative research that occasionally mentions the existence of 'malfunctioning councils'.[16]

In concluding this particular section there are two points that should be made. The first is that the TUC study group essentially took a positive view of the operation of works councils in Germany, although, as we shall note later, it was recognized that a simple transplant of the arrangements to Britain was not a feasible option. And the second point is that the German industrial relations system is currently experiencing considerable internal debate concerning its own future direction and shape, the outcome of which will clearly have considerable implications for the role of works councils. This debate has arisen as a result of a downturn in economic growth (real GDP declined by nearly 2 per cent in 1993), a rise in unemployment, large-scale job losses in the manufacturing sector, and the substantial rise in the public sector deficit (as a result of the costs of unification). Employers advocating the need for reform of the industrial relations system are overwhelmingly concerned with the relatively high level of labour costs in Germany. Table 7.3 provide some relevant evidence in this regard.

The concern about the level of labour costs in Germany has translated into an employer demand (particularly among small and medium-sized organizations) for more decentralized bargaining arrangements, with the maintenance of industry-wide collective bargaining arrangements being the particular target of

Table 7.3 *Comparative labour costs, early 1990s*

| | Average hourly compensation (US$)[a] | | | |
| | 1991 | 1992 | 1993 | 1994 |
| --- | --- | --- | --- | --- |
| *Europe, high* | | | | |
| Western Germany | 22.91 | 25.38 | 25.56 | 25.93 |
| Switzerland | 21.69 | 23.21 | 22.66 | 23.00 |
| Belgium | 19.83 | 22.23 | 21.38 | 21.69 |
| Norway | 21.63 | 23.03 | 20.20 | 20.42 |
| Austria | 18.15 | 20.41 | 20.20 | 19.94 |
| Netherlands | 18.44 | 20.48 | 20.16 | 19.75 |
| Denmark | 18.26 | 20.02 | 19.12 | 19.55 |
| *Europe, medium* | | | | |
| Sweden | 22.15 | 24.59 | 17.91 | 18.20 |
| Finland | 21.25 | 19.92 | 16.56 | 17.25 |
| France | 15.26 | 16.89 | 16.31 | 16.53 |
| Italy | 18.60 | 19.60 | 15.97 | 15.79 |
| UK | 13.77 | 14.44 | 12.82 | 13.50 |
| Ireland | 12.08 | 13.37 | 11.80 | 12.10 |
| Spain | 12.20 | 13.37 | 11.53 | 11.14 |
| *Europe, low* | | | | |
| Greece | 6.82 | 7.46 | 6.81 | 6.92 |
| Portugal | 4.24 | 5.17 | 4.60 | 4.19 |

[a] Includes non-wage costs.

*Source*: Economist Intelligence Unit, 'European labour costs hold steady', *Business Europe*, 19 September, 1994, p. 2.

their criticism. The demand is for more flexibility in industry agreements and a greater capacity to develop company- and plant-based terms and conditions of employment. Indeed, there are already references to individual companies leaving employers' associations, sectoral agreements being ignored, and firms and works councils reaching works agreements (the latter being technically illegal).[17] More recently, it has been suggested that the official figure of 90 per cent of all employees covered by union-negotiated minimum rates may be down to 65 or 70 per cent (*Financial Times*, 22 November 1994). The outcome of this on-going debate will undoubtedly have implications for the future role of works councils. For instance one recent assessment of the system has suggested that:

> The centrifugal consequences for the German model will probably intensify. There will be scope for greater decentralization and more actors, for a wider variety of patterns and coalitions. The works councils will have to extend their participation in the procedural regulation of day-to-day activities and job performance, and in doing so they will inevitably develop a co-management role. The unions will be forced to adjust their traditional structures and policies to these decentralizing tendencies; they will certainly have to increase their organizational knowledge and technical competence and – above all – improve their services to the works councils. Sooner or later the structural characteristics of the German model ... may be modified: the dual system may give way to a triple system of interest representation with sectoral bargaining between trade unions and employers associations, enterprise negotiations between work councils and management, and direct participation by work-groups with elected team leaders.[18]

## SEEKING TO TRANSPLANT WORKS COUNCILS FROM GERMANY?

If any attempt were made to transplant works councils from Germany to Britain, at least two questions would arise. First, would the councils operate in essentially the same way (that is, with similar patterns of behaviour and outcomes) in the two systems? And secondly, by what means would this transference process be brought about? In seeking to answer these two questions there are some complex issues to be thought through, with possibly some important trade-offs being involved.

In relation to the first question the TUC study group recognized that the positive experience with works councils in Germany derived in large measure from features of its wider industrial relations environment that had few counterparts in Britain.[19] These features included strong employers' associations and legislation extending negotiated terms and conditions of employment, industry-level collective bargaining arrangements, an industrial union structure and the general stability of industrial relations structures. These features have, in turn, facilitated union and works council interaction, made the issue of union recognition by individual employers essentially a non-issue, and helped ensure that the works councils operate as essentially joint problem-solving bodies.

This last factor has been particularly important as over the course of time employers have moved from their position of initial opposition to works councils to accepting and valuing their role; one recent survey reported that for nearly 80 per cent of managers the question was not whether they would co-operate with works councils, but how they should do so.[20] The fact that works councils in Germany have operated as joint problem-solving bodies (which has facilitated their widespread acceptance by employers) has in no small measure been due to the fact that the distributive side of the employment relationship (that is, wage bargaining) has been dealt with by industry-level collective bargaining. As one recent US assessment of works councils in Germany (and Europe more generally) has put it:

> External guarantees – be they social benefit guarantees, centrally determined wages, or rights based sanctions on job loss – in some measure render moot much intrafirm disagreement about the division of the surplus. By taking many intrafirm disputes over the surplus 'off the table' these guarantees underwrite internal co-operation and flexibility toward the joint goal of increasing firm performance.[21]

Interestingly, in view of the previous section, this line of argument would seem to imply that any future decline in industry-level collective bargaining in Germany could force works councils to take on more of a distributive bargaining agenda, which could result in councils acting less as joint problem-solving bodies. And this, in turn, could be a source of increased tension with employers.

The second question raised earlier was: by what means could any decision to transplant works councils to Britain be brought about? Should it involve legislation, or public policy encouragement via codes of practice, practitioner networks or tax incentives? The paper based on the TUC study group in Germany considered the case for the introduction of a statutory right for employees to establish works councils. However, it noted that any decision to go down the statutory route would require detailed consideration of a number of important questions: the nature of enforcement mechanisms/sanctions; the appropriate size threshold of organizations to which the legislation would apply; the relationship between unions and works councils; the fit with statutory recognition procedures; and the nature of employer responses to the proposals.

Once such details have been worked out, the obvious appeal of the statutory route is the speed with which structures can be put in place (that is, its potential for rapid diffusion); in this sense the institutional vacuum in the non-union sector could be relatively quickly filled by legislation providing for works councils. Moreover, the German experience indicates that works council legislation can be introduced in the face of employer opposition, and that such statutory arrangements can be increasingly accepted over time by employers as a result of accumulated positive experience; as was noted earlier, however, this positive experience was facilitated by larger features of the industrial relations system that have little counterpart in Britain. However, if such positive experience does not accumulate then this fact may provide a subsequent government with a rationale for repealing the relevant legislation.

Some indication of the potential value of legislation for introducing works councils (as integrative bargaining structures) in Britain can be gleaned from the experience with safety representatives and joint health and safety committees; these arrangements were facilitated by enabling legislation in 1974. This legislative underpinning was important in maintaining the presence of such arrangements throughout the 1980s, when union membership, recognition arrangements and collective bargaining coverage were all declining; specialist joint health and safety committees existed in 22 (23) per cent of establishments in 1984 (1990).[22] However, much more questionable is the extent to which such arrangements have constituted an effective force for change in workplace health and safety. For instance, some research in the chemical industry has suggested that:

> In many ways safety representatives and committees were not found to be the dominant force for change which many people had hoped or feared. Interviewees felt that their institution had probably raised the general level of awareness about safety matters within the workplace and had led to some issues being discussed, but that generally they had not had a profound effect on standards of health and safety. The views of managers ... have considerable bearing on this situation, as indeed do the views of the safety representatives themselves.[23]

For some commentators this sort of assessment could be improved by stronger legislation, spelling out more clearly the powers and duties of, for example, joint health and safety committees.[24] An alternative interpretation might be that there are some inherent limits to the extent to which one can legislate for integrative bargaining or joint problem-solving arrangements. There is clearly some validity to this argument, although the extent of this should not be exaggerated. Table 7.4 certainly suggests that some, but admittedly not all, features of an effective joint problem-solving body can be captured in legislation.

It might also be argued that any legislation or other public policy measures to encourage works councils in the non-union employment sector in Britain should be informed by current practice in this regard; the contention here being that such initiatives, if they did not diverge greatly from current practice, would be more likely to be acceptable to employers. Certainly company councils do exist in a number of non-union organizations in Britain. An illustrative example is provided in Box 7.1.

There are also company councils operating in Japanese subsidiaries with single-union agreements. For instance, a recent study of one such organization indicates that the nature of the council's role has changed over time and, although the union role in the organization has not been obviously marginalized, the task of establishing a consensus culture has been far from straightforward.[25] It is this sort of longitudinal research concerning company councils in the non-union and union sectors that could pay major dividends in the context of discussions concern-

Table 7.4    *Features of an effective joint health and safety committee*

---

- The committee is viewed primarily by management, employees and unions as a vehicle for developing a joint problem-solving approach towards workplace health and safety.

- The objective characteristics (for example, how often they meet, who chairs them, etc.) of existing committees vary considerably, although frequent meetings, regular attendance, and a joint agenda are viewed by many commentators as important features of successful committees.

- To practitioners, effective committees are overwhelmingly characterized by the relative absence of 'them vs us' attitudes and a strong senior management commitment to the workings of the committee.

- The quality of the larger working relationship between employees, unions and management will strongly influence the workings of the committee.

- Workplace health and safety training is important for all committee members.

- For committees to be pro-active bodies, it is important that their agenda does not become essentially a loose collection or shopping list of health and safety complaints/grievances.

- Increasingly, the better committees are centring their agenda on the findings and implementation of prior health and safety audits.

---

*Source*: Based on P.B. Beaumont, 'Meeting of minds?', *Occupational Safety and Health*, 22 (11), 1992, pp. 34–7.

ing any future role for works councils in Britain. Table 7.5 highlight some of the leading features of company councils in seven organizations, five of which were non-union ones.

A similar, more recent study has been conducted of company councils in British organizations, although again the information is largely limited to information concerning the composition and terms of reference of the councils.[26] Clearly more research-based information concerning the evolution and changing nature of such councils over time, and the extent to which (and why) they are perceived as effective bodies (or not) by the various parties concerned, would be a useful input to any public policy discussions in the future.

## Box 7.1   *A non-union works council: an illustrative example*

This non-union foreign-owned plant in the electronics industry currently employs some 570 people. The plant began production in 1988, and the works (or 'members' ') council has been in operation since then. Currently there are 11 employee representatives on the council and 4 managers (including the managing director); it is always chaired by the personnel director. There are no restrictions (for example, minimum length of service) on who can be an employee representative, and originally representatives (covering all areas of the plant) were elected by a workforce ballot on an annual basis; but over time the ballots have been held on more of a two-yearly basis. Currently there are proposals to change these arrangements so as to have half the representative positions up for election each year; the hope here is to 'have both continuity and new ideas together'. The employee representatives meet by themselves on a monthly basis to draw up a list of agenda items for the monthly council meeting. This list is then passed to the personnel director, who will add any management items concerning business issues and the state of the site for the full monthly meeting. Individual grievances are the only item that is expressly excluded from the council's agenda; group grievances can, however, be raised. The annual wage increases are discussed in the council, but there is no question of negotiations taking place there. There is some concern among management that the agenda of the committee has become over time a large, rather loose and poorly prioritized shopping list of issues. As a consequence, it has been proposed that two external bodies should discuss with the representatives their perceived training needs and then establish a programme to meet such needs; this will be the first occasion on which the employee representatives have received any such training.

## SUMMARY

The case for adding works councils to the institutional arrangements of Britain is currently being discussed in certain quarters.

Table 7.5    *Leading features of company councils*

---

- Council meetings varied from quarterly to once a month, with some provision for special meetings during the pay review.
- Sub-committees existed in larger organizations and for specific subject areas.
- The councils consisted of a number of elected employee representatives (6–26) and several senior managers.
- In most instances the chairperson was a nominated member of senior management.
- The nature of the council's involvement in the annual pay review varied substantially, although the emphasis was very much on pay discussions as opposed to pay negotiations.
- Employee representatives were elected by a workforce ballot, with the representatives' term of office being from 1 to 3 years.
- A minimum length-of-service qualification for employee representatives and/or a good disciplinary record was frequently specified.
- The size of employee representative constituencies ranged from 12 to 50 employees.
- All employee representatives received some relevant training.

---

*Source*: IDS Study 437, July 1989.

This case is very largely based on German experience, where employees, unions and management appear relatively well satisfied with the operation of such arrangements.

However, important questions still remain as to the appropriate means of introducing more works councils into Britain, and whether such arrangements would operate in a similar manner to those in Germany. By definition, no clear-cut answers can be given to these questions at this stage, although the contents of this chapter have highlighted the following points for consideration in any future discussion of this matter.

- It will be important to ensure that works councils operate as essentially integrative bargaining mechanisms.
- There are some limits to the extent to which such a mode of operation can be brought about by legislation.
- More research concerning the actual operation of company

councils in the non-union sector would be a line of activity that would be worth actively pursuing.

This question of the future role of works councils in Britain will be returned to in the next chapter.

## REFERENCES

1  *IRS.Employment Trends*, 556, March 1994.
2  M. Hall, 'Works councils for the UK? Lessons from the German system', Warwick Papers in Industrial Relations 46, November 1993.
3  T.A. Kochan, L. Dyer and R. Batt, 'International human resource studies: a framework for future research', in D. Lewin, U.S. Mitchell and P.D. Sherer (eds), *Research Frontiers in Industrial Relations and Human Resources*, IRRA Research Volume, Madison, Wisconsin, University of Wisconsin, 1992, pp. 309–40.
4  P.B. Beaumont, *Change in Industrial Relations*, London, Routledge, 1990, p. 235.
5  W. Kendall, *The Labour Movement in Europe*, London, Allen Lane, 1975, pp. 128–9.
6  ILO, *Collective Bargaining*, Geneva, ILO, 1973, p. 35.
7  Kendall, *Labour Movement*, p. 126.
8  J.T. Addison, K. Kraft and J. Wagner, 'German works councils and firm performance', in B.E. Kaufman and M.M. Kleiner (eds), *Employee Representation: Alternatives and Future Directions*, IRRA Research Volume, Madison, Wisconsin, University of Wisconsin, 1993, p. 306.
9  Addison et al., 'German works councils', p. 310.
10  D. Jacobi, B. Keller and W.M. Jentsch, 'Germany: co-determining the future', in A. Ferner and R. Hyman (eds), *Industrial Relations in the New Europe*, Oxford, Blackwell, 1992, p. 232.
11  Jacobi et al., 'Germany: co-determining the future', p. 243.
12  Addison et al., 'German works councils', p. 310.
13  R.B. Freeman and J. Rogers, 'Who speaks for us? Employee representation in a non-union labor market', in Kaufman and Kleiner (eds), *Employee Representation*, p. 51.
14  Ibid.
15  Addison, et al., 'German works councils', pp. 322–34.
16  Freeman and Rogers, 'Who speaks for us?', p. 51.
17  *European Industrial Relations Review*, 245, June 1994.

18   Jacobi et al., 'Germany: co-determining the future', pp. 266–7.

19   Hall, 'Works councils for the UK?'

20   *European Industrial Relations Review*, 247, August 1994, p. 7.

21   Freeman and Rogers, 'Who speaks for us?', p. 45.

22   N. Millward, M. Stevens, D. Smart and W.R. Hawes, *Workplace Industrial Relations in Transition*, Aldershot, Dartmouth, 1992, p. 162.

23   S. Dawson, P. Willman, M. Bamford and A. Clinton, *Safety at Work: The Limits of Self Regulation*, Cambridge, Cambridge University Press, 1988, p. 85.

24   D. Walters, *Worker Participation in Health and Safety: A European Comparison*, London, Institute of Employment Rights, 1990.

25   G. Broad, 'Japan in Britain: the dynamics of joint consultation', *Industrial Relations Journal*, 25 (1), 1994, pp. 26–38.

26   IDS Study 561, September 1994.

# 8
# WHERE NEXT?

## INTRODUCTION

The basic aim of this book has been twofold. Firstly, to develop and elaborate the argument concerning both the sources and adverse consequences of an institutional vacuum emerging in the British industrial relations system. And secondly, to examine some of the institutional arrangements that can potentially help fill this vacuum and, at the same time, raise certain questions and issues concerning the various public policy instruments that can be involved in the processes of eliminating it.

In the course of Chapter 5 it was argued that Britain has historically been characterized by a failure to institutionalize and diffuse, at least on a reasonably comprehensive basis, various employment-management innovations designed to supplement and complement collective bargaining arrangements. The most sanguine interpretation of this historical pattern is that the strength of collective bargaining undermined both the incentive for and ability of these other arrangements to take hold. However, the 1980s experience would seem to call this interpretation strongly into question, given that the decline in collective bargaining has not been 'offset' by a sizeable natural diffusion process involving HRM practices, particularly in the non-union sector of employment. As a consequence it was argued that both the historical and contemporary institutionalization/diffusion failures in the employment-management area derive from a larger set of organizational arrangements and practices that accord relatively limited importance and priority to employment-management issues in organizational decision-making processes. In short, any public policy attempts to bring about change in the employment-management domain have to reach beyond the traditionally defined parameters of this domain. This particular theme is one of a number pursued in this final chapter which seeks to draw together a number of strands concerning the possibilities for change in the British system of industrial relations.

## DIFFERING PERSPECTIVES ON EMPLOYMENT-MANAGEMENT ISSUES

There is currently a great deal of public policy debate both within and across nations concerning the essential components of an effective competitive strategy. Table 8.1 indicates some of the recent initiatives contained in the Government's recent (May 1994) White Paper on Competitiveness. The notion of 'flexible' labour market arrangements is frequently central to many competitive strategy discussions. There is clearly considerable consensus across countries on the need for flexible labour market operations, but a great deal of variation in exactly what the notion of flexibility means in practice; such differing views were much in evidence at the G7 meeting in Detroit early in 1994 (*Financial Times*, 14 March 1994). To many commentators the essence of the flexibility debate involves the choice between (1) a high-wage/high-productivity model, emphasizing quality, training, etc., which is stimulated by rigidities in the external labour market (that is, the German approach) and (2) a low-labour-cost approach, characterized by the deregulation of the external labour market (that is, the UK/US approach).

The Conservative Government's notion of flexible labour market arrangements involves very much an acceptance of the neo-classical assumptions that (i) firms exist to maximize shareholder value, (ii) firms compete very largely on the basis of price and (iii) the labour factor is a cost of production that must be minimized as a route to competitive advantage. To Government spokesmen this approach has been an important engine of job creation, although critics worry about the quality of the jobs created, noting that many of them are part-time ones with 'inferior' terms and conditions of employment (*Financial Times*, 15 March 1994). As was noted in Chapter 5, the Government has undoubtedly introduced, with its deregulation approach, some new influences into the operation of the labour market since 1979: attempts to curb union power, the reduction of benefit payments relative to income from employment, privatization, etc. At the same time, however, it has reinforced (indeed accentuated) the long-standing employer commitment to a low-labour-cost competitive strategy.

Table 8.1 *New competitiveness initiatives*

1 *Education and training*
- £300m-worth of new measures to strengthen vocational training and education
- a new general diploma at GCSE level and new vocational options to be developed
- £100m for better careers guidance and work experience
- £100m for new accelerated apprenticeship for people aged 18 to 19
- £60m to train up to 24,000 key workers in small companies
- consultation on credits for 16- to 19-year-olds to purchase their own education

2 *Business links*
- business links scheme to be extended to provide back-up in the area of export, innovation, technology and design
- export consultants and innovation and technology counsellors to be placed in 70 business link centres

3 *Innovation*
- innovation credits, worth up to £1,000, for small firms to encourage use of outside experts
- new initiatives to strengthen links between universities and business
- six sectoral groups to be set up to work with the City to improve the flow of finance for innovation

4 *Late payment*
- Government departments to follow Confederation of British Industry's late payment code
- annual reports to include companies' payment records
- review to strengthen the informal small claims procedure

5 *Business finance*
- business angels scheme to be boosted
- aim of national coverage of a local brokerage system

6 *Regional aid*
- a regional challenge, based on the City Challenge model

7 *Transport*
- proposal to privatize the National Air Traffic Services
- a competition for privately financed trains for London Underground's Northern line

Table 8.1    *continued*

---

8    *Deregulation*

• acceptance of Health and Safety Commission's recommendations to remove 40 per cent of regulations affecting business

• consultation on simplified arbitration law and on increasing size of companies qualifying for accounting disclosure concessions

---

*Source*: *Financial Times*, 25 May 1994, p. 11.

The result is that a very narrow perspective is taken on the employment-management relationship as a route to competitive advantage, which is essentially confined to the neo-classical assumptions outlined above.

This limited perspective is apparent within Government economic policy-making circles, as is indicated by an examination of the changing position of the Department of Employment. This department emerged from the years of the Second World War as a relatively powerful government ministry, strongly committed to the maintenance of free collective bargaining arrangements. This position has been substantially eroded over the course of time by the sort of developments and changes listed in Table 8.2.

In short, over time the Department of Employment has lost its historical role as an advocate of an alternative (to the neo-classical) view of the employment-management relationship, an alternative view that historically was important in Government economic policy-making circles. This process of change has reached such a stage that the Engineering Employers' Federation has recently proposed that the Department of Employment should be abolished, with its remaining functions being hived off to the Department of Trade and Industry and the Department of Education (*Financial Times*, 25 April 1994).

The Government's support and encouragement of the traditional low-labour-cost competitive strategy in Britain reinforces, in turn, the traditional view of organizations, which emphasizes (1) the primacy of shareholder interests and (2) the importance of meeting short-run measures of financial performance. According to Thurow, the emphasis attached to short-run profit maximization by US firms is only exceeded by firms in Britain.[1] Thurow goes on to distinguish between the profit-maximizing firms of Britain and the USA ('consumer economics') and the strategic-conquest orientation (that is, of enhancing longer-run market share) of German and Japanese firms ('producer economics'). The competitive strategy of the latter firms generally accords much more priority and importance to the role of the employment-management relationship. Moreover the nature of the relationship is viewed and managed very differently in these two groups of organizations, with some of the leading manifestations of this difference being identified by Thurow as follows:

- Wage costs are to be minimized in profit-maximizing firms.
- Automation is associated with wage decreases in profit-maximizing firms, but wage increases in strategic-conquest ones.

Table 8.2 *The changing role of the Department of Employment*

---

The Department's traditional role:
In the period 1945–65, the Department was essentially an advocate of 'free collective bargaining'.

Challenges to this traditional role in the 1970s:
  (i) the issuing of a code of industrial relations practice to accompany the Industrial Relations Act 1971;
 (ii) the establishment of the Commission on Industrial Relations as the external agent of change in industrial relations;
(iii) the hiving off of the conciliation function with the establishment of ACAS; and
 (iv) the setting-up of the Manpower Services Commission and the Health and Safety Executive.

Further changes in the 1980s:
  (i) the production of documentation supporting the Government's industrial relations legislative programme;
 (ii) the Rayner and internal efficiency enquiries;
(iii) the deregulation of industry initiatives; and
 (iv) documentation critical of the social dimension of an integrated Europe.

---

*Source*: Adapted from M.R. Freedland, 'The role of the Department of Employment – twenty years of institutional change', in W. McCarthy (ed.), *Legal Intervention in Industrial Relations*, Oxford, Blackwell, 1992, pp. 274–95.

- There is less overall training in profit-maximizing firms, with the training being largely job-specific in nature and concentrated among management personnel.
- Bonus or performance-related pay is individual-based in profit-maximizing firms, but in strategic-conquest ones such arrangements are based on teams or the organization as a whole.
- The size of the wage/salary gap between senior managers and the average employee is much greater in profit-maximizing firms.[2]

These differences in competitive strategy are closely bound up with differences in the nature of 'corporate governance' arrangements. The body of literature on the latter has strongly emphasized the fact that hostile merger and acquisition activity is much more a feature of the UK and US systems than of Japan and continental Europe. Table 8.3 provides an outline view of some of the leading effects and causes of the relatively high level of mergers and acquisitions in Britain.

One of the major points made in Table 8.3 concerns the limited efficiency of mergers as an external control device. This point has been made even more forcefully by other researchers. Kay, for instance, has argued that, taken as a whole, merger activity adds very little value, with both managers and markets tending to overestimate the resulting gains substantially.[3] More specifically, the available research variously indicates that:

- Hostile takeovers are a relatively costly form of external control.
- Takeovers are not always concentrated among poorly performing firms.
- The evidence of sustained, improved performance in the post-merger situation is relatively limited.[4]

In summary, we would appear to have the following situation: British firms accord a relatively high priority to shareholder interests and to meeting short-run financial measures of performance. Furthermore, the pursuit of a low-labour-cost competitive strategy, together with a threat of a hostile external takeover,

Table 8.3 *Some effects and causes of the shareholder model in Britain*

---

*Effects*

1 Management concentrates on short-run objectives.

2 Mergers/acquisitions, largely of a hostile nature, constitute the major form of external corporate control.

3 The high level of takeover activity results in a high turnover of executives.

4 The efficiency and effectiveness of takeovers as an external control strategy is questionable.

5 The scope for speculative investments and individual firm initiatives is relatively high.

*Causes*

1 Dispersal of shareholdings across a sizeable range of institutional and individual investors.

2 The relative absence of cross-shareholding by firms.

3 The relative absence of cross-representation on company boards.

---

In the UK more than 60 per cent of issued equity is held by financial and non-financial corporations; less than 4 per cent of this is attributable to the non-financial corporate sector. Nearly all is held by pension funds and life assurance companies on behalf of private investors.

In the UK, in two-thirds of the largest 200 companies there is no single shareholder with a holding in excess of 10 per cent of issued equity.

*Source*: Based on T. Jenkinson and C. Mayer, 'The assessment: corporate governance and corporate control', *Oxford Review of Economic Policy*, 8 (3), 1992, pp. 1–10; also Centre for Economic Performance, LSE, 'Review of the year's work 1992–93', Discussion Paper 174, 1993.

means that short-run financial considerations dominate internal management decision-making processes. Conversely, there is limited importance accorded to the employment-management relationship, which has slowed the response to the decline of collective bargaining in the sense of producing a limited diffusion of HRM practices. As a consequence, the institutional vacuum that has emerged in the industrial relations system can only be comprehensively addressed by public policy measures orientated to changing the larger features of British firms.

## SOME REFORM PROPOSALS FOR 'SHORT-TERMISM'

The sharp trade-off between meeting shareholder interests and employee interests in British firms has been highlighted in a recent press report concerning the poor state of employee morale in British Telecom (BT), Europe's most profitable company (*Financial Times*, 7 November 1994). It is this sort of trade-off relationship which may lie at the heart of some recent survey-based research that has suggested that HRM practices are associated with an improved productivity performance, but with a poorer climate of industrial relations and a higher staff turnover rate.[5]

In recent years a number of well-known management writers have urged that British and US firms need to reduce the priority they attach to shareholder interests, and conversely increase the importance accorded to employee interests.[6] Obviously, any tangible proposals along these lines will encounter very considerable 'political' opposition from the business community. Moreover, some academics have argued that any attempt to move from an 'outsider' system of corporate governance (US and UK) to an 'insider' one (Japan and continental Europe) needs to recognize that:

> It is difficult to shift from an outsider to an insider regime. An insider system relies on self-monitoring of the corporate sector by the corporate sector. It is a network in which companies own and monitor each other. Such a system makes it difficult for any one company to try to shift over to such an arrangement by itself: there is a co-ordination problem. What is harder is to establish a system by which companies invest in each other and take controlling shareholdings. The only way in which this currently appears feasible in the UK is via cross-shareholdings. Companies can purchase reciprocal shareholdings in each other and take seats on each other's boards. That helps to relieve both the financing and control problems of moving away from an outsider system. However it would take time for a corporate sector to establish an insider system through cross-shareholding.[7]

This being said, the 'short-termism' of British companies, as reflected in, for example, comparatively high dividend payments, has become a source of concern and discussion in certain political circles. For instance, the House of Commons Trade and Industry Committee have urged institutional investors to adopt a more flexible approach to corporate dividend payments (*Financial Times*,

3 May 1994). The latest indications are, however, that the Treasury has abandoned its proposed review of whether dividend payments of UK companies are too high (*Financial Times*, 24 November 1994). However, the announcement of a 75 per cent increase in the salary of the Chief Executive of British Gas has been a source of some embarrassment to the present Government, and has stimulated discussion of possible measures to curb increases of this magnitude (*Financial Times*, 21 November 1994). The Labour Party have produced a document which has variously suggested that:

- Hostile takeover bids should have to demonstrate that they would be in the 'public interest'.
- Tax changes should encourage long-term holding of shares.
- Better information should be provided for pension fund trustees.
- There should be statutory reporting of long-term indicators of corporate strength in annual reports.
- There should be a review of the case for establishing a minimum legal standard for the composition of company boards.
  (*Financial Times*, 1 June 1994)

Academics have also proposed changes in this area. For instance, Charkham has suggested that a Royal Commission should be established to examine the role and effects of hostile takeovers.[8] Table 8.4 contains another set of relevant proposals concerning takeovers and the short-termism issue.

If the Labour Party lead in the opinion polls in the summer of 1994 (20–33 percentage points) translates into an election victory, then some of the proposals above are likely to be actively on the political agenda in the not too distant future. The prime purpose of these proposals is to enhance economic efficiency and competitive performance; but by reducing the strength of short-run financial considerations in management decision-making processes they can, conversely, potentially increase the priority attached to employment-management issues in such decisions. Labour Party proposals for a training levy/rebate system to encourage workforce training could also be influential in this regard (*Financial Times*, 28 September 1994).

Table 8.4   *Policy proposals to address the takeover process*

---

- All contested takeovers above a given size should automatically be referred to the Monopolies and Mergers Commission.
- The onus of proof that such contested bids are in the public interest should be shifted to the predator.
- The definition of the public interest should only include two criteria: competition and economic efficiency.
- Voting rights attached to more than 1 per cent of shares in issue of a given company should not be vested until a year after purchase; in the interim period voting rights would be exercised by the directors of the company.
- A reduction in the threshold at which a predator is obliged to make an offer to all shareholders from 29.9 per cent to 14.9 per cent.
- An overhaul of trust law relating to pension funds to provide a clearer framework for the legal ownership of the pension fund itself.

---

*Source*: 'Takeovers and short-termism in the UK', Industrial Policy Paper No. 3, London, Institute for Public Policy Research, 1990, p. 7.

As well as advocating these larger corporate-level changes, I would also argue that there is a need to deal with the institutional vacuum in the non-union employment sector more directly. And this will require legislation and/or other public policy interventions concerned with collective bargaining, HRM practices and/or works councils. Obviously the success of any initiatives along these lines will be assisted if they can tap into, enhance and accelerate any 'positive' on-going tendencies in the system at large. It is this issue that we now turn to address.

## ANY FERTILE GROUND?

As Pfeffer has argued in the US context,[9] one of the potentially most important positive tendencies (from the point of view of raising the priority attached to the employment–management relationship in competitive strategy) is the so-called quality movement. The current interest of many organizations in seeking BS 5750 accreditation, and introducing continuous improvement or total quality management (TQM) programmes, is an indication of some attempt to reorientate competitive strategies away from the traditional low-labour-cost orientation. Unfortunately, we lack a comprehensive and representative database that could tell us just how widespread are such programmes. Moreover, current initiatives along these lines have not been without their critics. For instance, various commentators have questioned the rigour of the BS 5750 accreditation procedures (*Financial Times*, 21 June 1994), suggested that in practice employment-management considerations do not receive the attention suggested by the rhetoric of such programmes,[10] and that evidence concerning their effects and performance is little more than anecdotal in nature.[11]

This being said, quality programmes, with their emphasis on workforce training, team working and employee involvement and consultation, can potentially be spread or diffused to a relatively wide range of organizations. The HRM practices associated with quality programmes can be diffused, firstly, by the availability of prestigious national awards, and secondly, by the changing nature of supply-chain management relationships. In the USA the Malcolm Baldrige Quality Award (administered since 1988 by the Department of Commerce and the American Society for Quality Control) has been widely held to constitute a powerful diffusion instrument:

> It is important to understand the Baldrige Award because it has already affected the behaviour of thousands of managers across the US. In the first five rounds since its inception in 1988, approximately 500 applicants have entered the competition. However, many more companies have been influenced by the Baldrige competition than the numbers of applicants indicate. In 1992, for example, 240,000 companies requested copies of the award criteria and application. Moreover, the Award has spread networking and benchmarking among firms by requiring winners to respond to requests for information. Baldrige winners have given hundreds of lectures and conferences to managers from other firms interested in replicating successful techniques.[12]

A European Quality Award also exists, and in early 1994 a new quality award for 'excellence in the application of total quality management (TQM)' was established in the UK. The criteria and weightings involved in this award are as follows:

- leadership (10 per cent)
- people management (9 per cent)

- policy and strategy (8 per cent)
- resources (9 per cent)
- processes (14 per cent)
- people (employee) satisfaction (9 per cent)
- customer satisfaction (20 per cent)
- impact on society (6 per cent)
- business results (15 per cent).[13]

It is not difficult to envisage HRM specialists arguing that people-management and employee satisfaction are under-weighted in this award. Nevertheless, the award has considerable potential to help diffuse a competitive orientation in which HRM practices are an explicit element. And a process of diffusion of quality approaches involving HRM practices by a second route is already under way, as a result of changes in the approach to supply-chain management relationships. For example, organizations that have gone down the quality improvement route have frequently reduced the size of their supplier base, raised the quality demands on their remaining suppliers, audited them and established supplier-development programmes. This process has invariably impacted on the working arrangements and practices of the supplier organizations, with increased levels of workforce training being particularly apparent in this regard.[14] The contents of Box 8.1 indicate that the extent of 'induced change' can extend beyond workforce training in some cases.

The potential for diffusing best practice quality approaches via this route has been increasingly recognized by a number of regional development agencies and bodies which have established customer–supplier networks. Indeed a non-profit-making body (Partnership Sourcing Ltd) was set up as part of a joint CBI–DTI initiative in 1990 to promote the concept of partnership sourcing in the UK. These sorts of initiatives have still to prove their worth, although they do usefully illustrate the fact that public policy instruments to diffuse employment-management innovations are not simply a matter of legislatively-based initiatives.

A second development worthy of note is the appearance of certain 'best practice' industrial relations models and guidelines in recent years. The contents of these documents seem to constitute, at least implicitly, a recognition (in certain informed practitioner and policy-making circles) of the fact that the introduction of

HRM practices (as part of a management change initiative) has not been handled particularly well. For instance, in 1992 the IPA issued a consultative document entitled 'Towards Industrial Partnership', which urged a new approach to union–management relations in Britain. In essence the document urged the parties to agree the following joint aims:

1   a joint commitment to the success of the enterprise, with the interests of employees, customers, suppliers, shareholders and the community all being taken into account;

---

**Box 8.1   *Supplying the motor vehicle industry: HRM change***

This non-union organization has some 350 employees. It has obtained BS 5750 accreditation, which has met the needs of most of its customers, but its leading customers are in the vehicle manufacturing industry. These major customers have during the course of the 1980s introduced quality improvement programmes of their own, with a strong emphasis on employee involvement.  And they, in turn, have sought similar changes from this supplier organization, with these demands for change being reflected in both the auditing instruments and supplier-development programmes of the customers. As a consequence, the supplier organization has from the late 1980s established two works councils (one for manufacturing, one for administration), and introduced bi-monthly team briefing arrangements and a performance appraisal process that emphasizes the identification of training/development needs. Most significantly of all, it has recently introduced cell working arrangements whereby production is split into product cells; as a result, small teams of workers are responsible for their own range of products from raw material stage to finished product. The supplier organization freely concedes that this change in production working would not have come about in the absence of the new quality audits of their customers in the vehicle manufacturing industry. Currently they are developing a supplier-development programme of their own that is looking for complementary changes from their suppliers.

---

2　a joint effort to build trust via openness, improved education, communication and information-sharing; and

3　a joint declaration recognizing the legitimate role of each party.

In order to give tangible expression to this partnership approach, management would need to increase its commitment to employment security, to be prepared to share the gains of any resulting success and to recognize the importance of employee rights to information, consultation and representation. At the same time, the unions would need to be committed to job flexibility, representation of the workforce as a whole, and acceptance of employee-involvement methods.

More recently, a document was produced by a union–management working party convened by ACAS (Wales) entitled 'Best Practice in Industrial Relations'. This document, which was based on the experience of five companies and four union representatives involved in the processes of organizational change, produced a set of guidelines, the essence of which is set out in Table 8.5.

It is unlikely that many employment-management specialists (be they academics or practitioners) would seriously disagree with the substantive content of such documents. However, if such documents are to constitute useful diffusion instruments they need to appreciate the lessons of history. For example, in the years immediately after the Second World War the Anglo-American

Table 8.5　*Guidelines for organizational change*

---

1　Recognize that a challenge to the present system exists.

2　Evolve a vision of the actions needed to meet it.

3　Prepare the ground for its successful implementation.

4　Identify the benefits available to those affected by it.

5　Recruit commitment to the new objectives and approaches.

6　Accept that making changes is everyone's responsibility.

7　Create space for the union(s) to contribute to the change.

8　Create mechanisms for exchanging and assessing new ideas.

9　Facilitate the unions to make a constructive response.

10　Keep faith to sustain mutual trust and confidence.

---

*Source*: ACAS Wales, *Best Practice in Industrial Relations*, 1994.

Council on Productivity was established, joint study teams from Britain visited companies in America, and 47 reports were produced and circulated within industry. However, an assessment of this exercise concluded that 'overall it would seem the Government's attempt to use the AACP to engage the enthusiasm of employers and unions for the productivity drive failed. There is little evidence the AACP reports had much impact *except upon the already converted*' (my emphasis).[15]

An essentially similar conclusion was reached in Chapter 5, where codes of practice and inter-firm networks were examined as instruments of diffusion. Accordingly, if the contents of the above documents are to bring about any substantive change they must break out of the long-standing problem of speaking to the converted. This means that much more attention needs to be given in public policy circles to questions such as the following: (1) what are the particular organizations that can constitute useful role models in such publications; and (2) how can the message reach organizations that are not regular attenders at specialist employment-management conferences and workshops? For instance, some of the analysis in Chapter 5 (concerning employee share-ownership schemes) pointed to the importance of *industry-*based role models in the adoption and diffusion process. These are important questions in the design and dissemination of such documents, which have not received the attention that their importance warrants.

In short, the so-called 'quality movement' is associated with certain principles, practices and mechanisms that have the potential to help spread HRM practices more widely throughout the system. Codes of practice, inter-firm networks, benchmarking visits, quality awards, changing customer–supplier relationships can all, in the absence of legislation, play a role as diffusion mechanisms. But for this to occur (1) the employment–management relationship must be given more emphasis/priority in the underlying principles; (2) the processes of introducing such practices need to be given more attention by management; and (3) the diffusion process must reach organizations that historically have shown little tendency to innovate on their own initiative. For this situation to come about it will be essential to enact via legislation some of the earlier-noted measures designed to combat the traditional 'short-termism' of British organizations. Serious consideration should also be given to reviewing the experience with tax incentives in stimulating the take-up of employee share-ownership arrangements (see Chapter 5) and building on this experience by providing incentives for the adoption of other HRM practices.

ACAS is a body that can also make a potentially significant contribution to helping fill the institutional gap in the British industrial relations system. The recent legislatively-based changes in its terms of reference could allow it to direct its activities increasingly towards the non-union employment sector. Obviously a suggestion along these lines needs to recognize the reality of budget constraints (the ACAS budget is scheduled to be cut by some 15 per cent in the period 1993/4–1996/7), the necessity to maintain good working relationships with the unions, and the fact that their favoured joint problem-solving approach is obviously facilitated by the existence of employee representatives. This being said, a recent survey of the ACAS advisory function noted that 'levels of problem resolution and customer satisfaction are even higher where participative methods are used in the non-union sector than they are where unions are recognized'.[16] This particular finding would seem to enhance the case for ACAS more vigorously to market its in-depth advisory work in the non-union sector.

## THE EUROPEAN DIMENSION AND WORKS COUNCILS

Further change in the British industrial relations system is likely to stem from its involvement in the European Union. The present Government's opting out from the social dimension of Europe is well known, although the longer-term viability of this decision has been questioned; certainly a future Labour Government has indicated its intention to opt in. However, despite the current Government's position, the general expectation is that European Union initiatives will increasingly influence industrial relations developments in Britain.[17] The specific effects typically mentioned in this regard include the increased exchange of information between unions across national boundaries and the increased influence of certain European practices and arrangements (for example works councils, co-ordinated bargaining) in the discussions and agendas of British Unions. Currently a great deal of union interest is centred on the European directive on works councils, which provides that every company or industrial group employing at least 1,000 workers in the EU, and with at least 100 workers in two member states, will have to introduce a works council. It is estimated that at least 60 UK-based multinational companies will be covered by this directive, although they do not have to include their UK employees in the arrangements as a result of Britain's opt-out from the social chapter. However, the TUC and individual unions in Britian have been actively working with their counterparts in mainland Europe to try to ensure that British employees are included in the coverage of the resulting arrangements. In mid-1994 United Biscuits (which has 35,000 UK employees) was reported to be the first UK multinational to have accepted the principle of including British employees in the coverage of a European works council (*Financial Times*, 17 June 1994).

Given the institutional vacuum in the non-union sector, there is another European-level development that is potentially of very considerable importance. In Britain the legal obligation on employers to consult and inform employee representatives is much weaker than in mainland Europe, (1) being limited to situations where unions are recognized and (2) covering only disclosure of information for collective bargaining purposes, redundancy consultation, consultation over business transfers and health and safety. The UK's application of the 1975 collective redundancies directive and the 1977 transfers of undertakings directive has been criticized on the grounds that it does not apply in situations where unions are not recognized. Accordingly, as Hall has observed:

> The European Commission's view is that, with the repeal of the statutory recognition procedure in 1980, confining the obligation to consult over collective redundancies and business transfers to employers which recognize unions is no longer consistent with the requirements of the relevant EC directives. Infringement proceedings, if successful, could result in the European Court of Justice requiring the UK to make provision for the designation of employee representatives for the purposes of consultation under the two directives where there are no recognized unions.[18]

In June 1994 the European Court of Justice handed down its judgement in two cases in this area, upholding the bulk of the Commission's complaints and finding against the UK.[19] The effect of these two decisions is potentially very substantial for employment legislation in Britain, which will now have to provide for the designation of worker representatives for consultation purposes on such matters in non-union establishments. The major question will obviously be whether such legislation will provide for standing representative structures (which can assume a wider role over time), such as works councils, or more temporary, *ad hoc* structures. Following these judgements, at the 1994 meeting of the TUC an interim report ('Representation at Work') was presented which sought to 'integrate the idea of statutory representative bodies embracing all employees in establishments without recognized unions with the proposal for a step-by-step procedure whereby trade unions can secure recognition'. In seeking to build on the legislative response of the Government to these European-level judgements, the union movement needs to be particularly mindful of the following observations of one TUC officer:

> Some employers have signed up to the belief that a successful company must be union free. Others may take a more pragmatic line, negotiating with trade unions where they have to but taking the view that trade unions are an impediment to change. Finally there are those employers who are committed to a partnership approach, reject the Government's ideology and recognise that co-operation is the most effective way to improve performance. If the trade union movement has a task in the next six years it is to shift a substantial body of opinion from the 'pragmatist' into the 'partnership' camp.[20]

In short, the unions need to recognize that an increasing number of employers believe that unions add little value, with some believing that they are actually counter-productive. These employer perceptions need to be taken on board when seeking to evolve a 'union model' for the future. Hyman has suggested that there are four emergent identities for unions in the future:[21] (1) the provider of services for individual employees (the friendly society being the ideal type); (2) the productivity coalition, in which a co-operative union–management relationship is involved; (3) the political exchange model, in which interaction with the Government as social partner is important; and (4) the populist campaigning model, in which the union is part of a broader social movement. Given the current and future difficulties facing unions in Britain, and indeed many other advanced industrialized economies, it is hard to believe that a union movement will be able to rely on only one of these models to guarantee its future.[22] However, in opting for a mixture of these models, it will be absolutely essential for the British union movement to place a great deal of emphasis on model (2). That is, the union movement will have increasingly to demonstrate and publicize their strong commitment to a joint problem-solving relationship with management that is reflected in both the collective bargaining relationship and in their position with regard to HRM practices; this was one of the main arguments of Chapter 6.

The active pursuit of this approach will be essential in attempting to reduce the extent of current employer opposition to unions, which is reducing the coverage of collective bargaining and limiting the extent of union involvement in the introduction and operation of HRM practices. This being said, one has to admit that the pursuit of this route will not be without difficulties and problems, and certainly cannot be viewed as providing a guarantee of the unions' future. As was argued in earlier chapters, moving closer to management does risk the unions disrupting relations with their rank-and-file members, a possible development that needs to be watched and tackled through important internal union adjustments, for instance in their internal communications arrangements. Moreover, it needs to be recognized that the level of union density has been falling in Japan in recent times, despite its being widely regarded as the 'home' of co-operative union–management relationships.

To date, we have argued that the British industrial relations system has for long had a poor record in institutionalizing and diffusing employment-management innovations. However, this poor record has become more noticeable and of more concern as the traditional centrepiece of the system, collective bargaining, has declined. Moreover, this poor diffusion record stems at heart from the larger competitive strategy and management decision making structure of British organizations. Accordingly, it is in this larger strategy and structure area that reform must be initiated, rather than in the conventionally defined industrial relations domain. This being said, the more industrial relations–HRM specific issues noted above are important complementary agenda items.

## WHAT IS THE LIKELIHOOD THAT CHANGE WILL COME ABOUT?

In urging reform and change along these lines, it is only appropriate to ask whether it is likely to come about. Will there be a change of government? Will the new government place a relatively high priority on change along these lines? There are clearly a number of uncertainties when considering these sorts of questions. As Sisson has pointed out,[23] the relative performance of the British and German economies in the next few years will be particularly important. If the UK deregulated labour market approach is viewed as a significant source of job growth and continues to attract a substantial number of foreign-based organizations wishing to establish subsidiaries in Europe, while the German economy (with its social partnership approach and high labour costs) does not resume its role as the economic power of Europe, then the prospects of both electoral and organizational change will be reduced.

The present UK Government can obviously draw considerable comfort from the recent decision of Samsung to establish operations in Britain (*Financial Times*, 18 October 1994) and from some of the findings in the European Commission's Sixth Report on Employment in Europe (*Financial Times*, 15 September 1994). The latter, for instance, noted that low pay was a relatively minor source of poverty in the UK compared to most EU countries, and that the non-wage-labour costs imposed by government harmed the employment prospects of low-paid workers less in the UK than in the rest of the EU. There is also the possibility that the employment legislation programme emerging from Europe in the next few years will not be as comprehensive or broad-ranging as was being suggested in the late 1980s (*Financial Times*, 2 November 1994). If this is in fact the case, then union movements like that in Britain may not find the 'lifeline' from Brussels quite as powerful and influential as it was expected, or hoped, that it would be.

However, the position in Germany will also be particularly important. For example, Visser has argued that 'the big question for the future of trade unions in Europe is ... whether the German model will survive'.[24] To date the German model has survived the decline in corporatist arrangements and the pressures of decentralization and flexibility. But the latter pressures are very much on the increase (see Chapter 7) in response to the problems of declining macro-economic performance, the costs of unification, and employer concerns about the level of labour costs. For instance, a recent report suggested that effective hourly pay in West German manufacturing increased by 25 per cent between 1990 and 1993, whereas productivity rose by only 8 per cent (*Financial Times*, 21 November 1994).

The ability to adapt successfully to these enhanced pressures is not only important for the unions in Germany. It is also of major importance for practitioners and researchers elsewhere, who, as here, favour the competitive strategy, corporate governance and social partnership approach to labour market arrangements that are the traditional hallmark of the German model. The other 'role model' for this orientation is, of course, Japan, and here some concerns and changes in the system suggest some movement away from the traditional competitive strategy, with its strong HRM underpinnings. For instance, the level of union density continues to fall, individual performance-related pay arrangements are becoming more common in the finance sector, employment security commitments are being questioned, and traditional inter-company networks and cross-share-holding arrangements are loosening (*Financial Times*, 30 November 1994).

## BEYOND BRITAIN?

This book has primarily been concerned with changes and possible reforms in the British industrial relations system. However, the book began by noting that falls in the level of union density, and to a lesser extent in collective bargaining coverage, had characterized a number of advanced industrialized economies in recent years (Introduction, Table A). It is to this comparative theme that we now return.

A number of the themes, issues and concerns raised in this book are clearly not unique to Britain. This is well evidenced by the existence of a number of important union debates in countries other than Britain in recent years. For example, in the Netherlands the level of union density fell from some 36.6 per cent of employees in employment in 1978 to 27.1 per cent in 1986. Initially the unions responded by (1) seeking to improve the range of services to individual members and (2) targeting recruitment efforts more at part-time and women workers.[25] More recently, the two main union confederations have proposed to increase the efficiency of the union movement by establishing 'clusters' of affiliated unions, where the emphasis will be on enhancing the level of inter-union co-operation. In addition the unions have had to respond to the increasing decentralization tendencies of the industrial relations system in the Netherlands. Decision-making and bargaining are increasingly orientated to the sectoral and company levels, where unions have been traditionally weak. As a consequence, unions are seeking to forge closer, more co-operative links with works councils at these more decentralized levels of decision-making.

In Ireland the overall level of union density fell from some 55.2 per cent of the workforce in 1980 to 43.1 per cent in 1987. This was an important part of the background to the decision in the early 1990s of the Irish Congress of Trade Unions to commission two management consultants to examine changing forms of work organization and the implications they raised for trade unions. This work included twelve case studies of organizations in Ireland and discussions with union representatives in Germany and Sweden. The report essentially outlined five options for unions in responding to such organizational changes:

1  opposition;
2  allowing for local response (that is, having local representatives decide on a case-by-case basis);
3  adopting a minimalist approach (that is, one of union co-operation, given certain assurances);
4  adopting a pro-active approach; and
5  actively promoting changes, but with their own agendas.

The various benefits and risks associated with these differing options are set out in Table 8.6.

The report rejected the opposition and local response options, and recommended a policy based on the choice of the last three options (minimalist, pro-active and active promotion), with the particular option or approach being made on a company-by-company basis, depending on (1) the current and historical relationship between management, employees and unions; (2) the business circumstances of the individual company; and (3) the quality, depth and likely level of management commitment to the new work organization.

The report then went on to identify and highlight the implications for unions of pursuing the recommended options, with the major implications discussed being:

• trade union policy in areas such as rewards, work organization and participation;

Table 8.6 *Benefits and risks associated with options for trade union response*

| Option | Benefits | Risks |
|---|---|---|
| Opposition | maintains traditional adversarial approach<br><br>no need for union to adapt or change | unions bypassed by management<br><br>members questioning relevance and value of union membership<br><br>miss opportunity to be involved in QWL<br><br>damage to external perception of Ireland |
| Local response only | allows issues to be addressed without having a formal policy<br><br>maintains adversarial position nationally, while presenting a 'positive' response locally<br><br>no blurring of traditional IR agenda<br><br>no need for unions to change or adapt | wide variety of local practices<br><br>no support or guidance from trade unions<br><br>reacting rather than influencing management proposals<br><br>QWL initiative remains with management |
| Minimalist approach | provides clear policy and guidelines<br><br>provides framework for local officials and members<br><br>maintains uniformity of approach | takes no account of local practices<br>– existing relationships<br>– reasons for and scope of initiatives<br><br>limits scope of local officials to develop optimum solution<br><br>could be perceived as negative, if conditional upon achieving 'up-front' agreements |

Table 8.6   *continued*

| Option | Benefits | Risks |
|---|---|---|
| Positive approach | allows for a tailor-made approach | could blur traditional 'us and them ' relationships |
| | allows unions to optimize their level of input | blurring of traditional bargaining agenda |
| | opportunity for greater involvement of members | undermining of union solidarity |
| | builds member identification with union | variety of local outcomes |
| | more involved in shaping final outcomes | |
| Actively promote, but with own agenda | more involved in setting the agenda | could be perceived as 'doing management's job' |
| | seen to address wider member needs | undermining of union solidarity |
| | closely involved in ongoing monitoring | |

*Source*: Irish Congress of Trade Unions, *New Forms of Work Organisation: Options for Unions*, 1990, p. 44.

- the need for high levels of involvement of local officials and individual members in the specific detail of the policy agenda at enterprise level;
- the need to manage the interaction with companies in work organization in a flexible problem-solving manner;
- the need to re-evaluate existing internal union structures and processes to ensure effective support for full-time officials and workplace representatives;
- the development of the knowledge and skills of officials and members; and
- the development of additional and alternative methods of communication with their members.

What seems clear at the present time is that there are a number of *economic* influences that are common across national systems of industrial relations, and that virtually all of these are unfavourable to the maintenance, much less the enhancement, of existing levels of union organization. The obvious factors or influences here are changes in the composition of the workforce, increasingly international product markets, more competitive product markets, the pace of technological change, the growth of low-wage competition from newly industrializing economies, shorter product life cycles, privatization, etc.

This being said, changes in the level of union density varied considerably between national systems, and the overall level of collective bargaining coverage held up rather better in many systems in the 1980s than might have been expected (see Introduction, Table A). In general it would appear that historical and contemporary *political*, rather than economic, forces are the ones most likely to be favourable to the continued maintenance of existing levels of union organization. That is, systems characterized by a combination of a social partnership tradition (that is, centralized systems with a non-adversarial tradition) and a left-of-centre government in office would seem to have much better prospects for maintaining union organization and collective bargaining arrangements. But even here there are causes for union concern. For example, in Australia union density fell during the years when a Labour government was in office and co-operation between the government and the unions was being strongly emphasized.[26]

More generally, there are arguably growing limits to what even a sympathetic government can do, or is willing to do, to help unions. For instance, the freedom of manoeuvre for any one government in an increasingly interdependent economic world is arguably being reduced. Moreover, if the economy concerned is experiencing performance problems, then the government will undoubtedly face enhanced employer demands for cost control, decentralization, flexibility and the introduction of individual-employee-centred HRM practices. It would also appear that at least some left-of-centre parties are seeking to enhance their electoral prospects by opening up more ground between themselves and the union movement. The extent to which US unions have gained from the recent election of a Democratic President is perhaps instructive in this regard. Finally, it should be recognized that levels of union organization and collective bargaining coverage are being kept up in a number of countries by legislation- and regulation-based support measures: the unions are involved in administering unemployment benefits, or the results of collective bargaining are extended by legislation to non-union employers. However, a combination of macro-economic difficulties and the election of a government unsympathetic to the union movement can certainly place such support measures at risk, as the recent experience in New Zealand so graphically illustrates.

In summary, it is difficult to believe that the issues discussed here in relation to the British industrial relations system will not feature, albeit to differing degrees, on the agenda of researchers, practitioners and policy-makers in a number of other systems in the future.

## REFERENCES

1   L.C. Thurow, 'Who owns the twenty-first century?', *Sloan Management Review*, Spring, 1992, p. 8.
2   Ibid., pp. 8–10.
3   J. Kay, *Foundations of Corporate Success*, Oxford, Oxford University Press, 1993, pp. 146–50.
4   Ibid. Also T. Jenkinson and C. Mayer, 'The assessment: corporate governance and corporate control', *Oxford Review of Economic Policy*, 8 (3), 1992, p. 19.
5   Employment Policy Institute, Economic Report 8 (3), May, 1994.
6   See, for example, C. Handy, *The Empty Raincoat*, London, Hutchinson, 1994, Chapters 8 and 9, and R. Waterman, *The Frontiers of Excellence*, London, Nicholas Brealey, 1994.
7   Jenkinson and Mayer, 'The assessment', p. 19.
8   J. Charkham, *Keeping Good Company: A Study of Corporate Governance in Five Countries*, Oxford, Oxford University Press, 1994.
9   J. Pfeffer, *Competitive Advantage Through People*, Boston, Mass., Harvard Business School, 1994, Chapter 9.
10   P.B. Beaumont, L.C. Hunter and R. Phayre, 'Human resources and Total Quality Management: some case study evidence', *Training for Quality*, 2 (1), 1994, pp. 7–13.
11   D.C. Wilson, *A Strategy of Change*, London, Routledge, 1992, pp. 92–103.

12  E. Appelbaum and R. Batt, 'Policy levers for high performance production systems', *International Contributions to Labour Studies*, 3, 1993, p. 8.
13  *IRS Employment Trends*, 555, March 1994.
14  P.B. Beaumont, L.C. Hunter and D. Sinclair, 'Customer–supplier relations and human resource management', mimeographed paper, University of Glasgow.
15  Quoted in P. Hennessy, *Never Again: Britain 1945–1951*, London, Vintage, 1993, p. 377.
16  I. Kessler and J. Purcell, 'Evaluation of the ACAS in-depth advisory service: final report', Oxford, Institute for Employee Relations, Templeton College, 1994, p. 19.
17  P. Blyton and P. Turnbull, *The Dynamics of Employee Relations*, London, Macmillan, 1994, pp. 307–15.
18  M. Hall, 'Works councils for the UK? Lessons from the German system', Warwick Papers in Industrial Relations 46, November 1993, p. 8.
19  *European Industrial Relations Review*, 246, July 1994.
20  'Employment relations 2000', Warwick Papers in Industrial Relations, 50, July 1994, p. 12.
21  R. Hyman, 'Changing trade union identities and strategies', in R. Hyman and A. Ferner (eds), *New Frontiers in European Industrial Relations*, Oxford, Blackwell, 1994, pp. 133–6.
22  R. Taylor, *The Future of the Trade Unions*, London, Deutsch, 1994.
23  K. Sisson, 'Personnel management: paradigms, practice and prospects', in K. Sisson (ed.), *Personnel Management*, 2nd edn, Oxford, Blackwell, 1994, p. 44.
24  J. Visser, 'European trade unions: the transition years', in Hyman and Ferner (eds), *New Frontiers*, p. 101.
25  *European Industrial Relations Review*, 240, July 1994.
26  E. Davis, 'Trade unionism in the future', in J.R. Niland, R.D. Lansbury and C. Verevis (eds), *The Future of Industrial Relations*, London, Sage, 1994, pp. 120–1.

# Index